THE
Farmer's Wife
SAMPLER QUILT

THE
Farmer's Wife
SAMPLER QUILT

*Letters from
1920s farm wives*
AND THE
111 blocks they inspired

LAURIE AARON HIRD

KRAUSE PUBLICATIONS
CINCINNATI, OHIO

mycraftivity.com
connect. create. explore.

www.fwmedia.com

in writing from the publisher, except by a reviewer who may quote brief passages in a review. Published by Krause Publications, an imprint of F+W Media, Inc., 4700 East Galbraith Road, Cincinnati, Ohio, 45236. (800) 289-0963. First Edition.

13 12 11 10 09   5 4 3 2 1

DISTRIBUTED IN CANADA BY FRASER DIRECT
100 Armstrong Avenue
Georgetown, ON, Canada L7G 5S4
Tel: (905) 877-4411

DISTRIBUTED IN THE U.K. AND EUROPE BY DAVID & CHARLES
Brunel House, Newton Abbot, Devon, TQ12 4PU, England
Tel: (+44) 1626 323200, Fax: (+44) 1626 323319
Email: postmaster@davidandcharles.co.uk

DISTRIBUTED IN AUSTRALIA BY CAPRICORN LINK
P.O. Box 704, S. Windsor NSW, 2756 Australia
Tel: (02) 4577-3555

Library of Congress Cataloging in Publication Data

Hird, Laurie Aaron
    The farmer's wife sampler quilt / Laurie Aaron Hird. -- 1st ed.
        p. cm.
    Includes bibliographical references and index.
    ISBN-13: 978-0-89689-828-8 (pbk. : alk. paper)
    ISBN-10: 0-89689-828-8 (pbk. : alk. paper)
    1. Patchwork. 2. Quilting. 3. Farmers' spouses. I. Farmer's wife. II. Title.
TT835.H532 2009
746.46--dc22
                                        2009018355

Edited by Jay Staten
Designed by Julie Barnett
Illustrations by Toni Toomey
Production coordinated by Matt Wagner
Photography by Adam Hand, Al Parrish and Dave Peterson

DEDICATED TO:

My dear husband Steven and the children the Lord has so graciously given to us:

Amy and her husband Adam, Elizabeth and her husband Jared, Ruthanne,

Timothy and his wife Katherine, Leah, Josiah, Stephen, Laura, Seth, Martha and Mary.

THANKS TO:

Nell Coons of Verona, Wisconsin, for understanding the 1922 theme and for her beautiful longarm machine quilting.

Julie Barnett, for her outstanding job in designing this book.

Carol Corrieri @ QuiltBook.com for many of the lovely reproduction fabrics used in this quilt. She even irons the fabric!

MANY, MANY GRATEFUL THANKS TO:

My editor, illustrator and dear friend, Toni Toomey, who believed in my vision for this book and went to bat for it.

Without her patient tutelage, hard work and determination, this book would never have been published. Thank you, Toni!

METRIC CONVERSION CHART

TO CONVERT	TO	MULTIPLY BY
inches	centimeters	2.54
centimeters	inches	0.4
feet	centimeters	30.5
centimeters	feet	0.03
yards	meters	0.9
meters	yards	1.1

TABLE *of* CONTENTS

THE QUILT BLOCKS

THE QUILT

The Changing American Culture of the 1920s

The year 1922 lies between two important events in American history. The first event was the end of World War I on November 11, 1918. The second was the Stock Market Crash of 1929 that plunged the world into the Great Depression. On the surface, this eleven-year period seems like a quiet time, but it was actually a time of political and technological changes that brought America great social change.

Two important amendments to the United States Constitution were enacted during this period. The Eighteenth Amendment, ratified in 1919, prohibited the use of alcohol; and most important to women, the Nineteenth Amendment, enacted in 1920, gave them the right to vote.

The 1920s saw Americans entertaining themselves in new ways as well. In 1920, the first commercial radio station, KDKA in Pittsburgh, went on the air. By 1922, over five hundred commercial stations were in operation, and by 1929, half of American homes boasted a radio. Because of radio's popularity, jazz music, which began in New Orleans during World War I, spread throughout the country. In 1922, silent pictures were extremely popular, with ticket sales of 40 million per week. But these days would soon be replaced by a new era beginning in 1927, when Al Jolson starred in the first "talkie" movie, *The Jazz Singer*.

For rural Americans especially, the popularization of the automobile meant that they were no longer confined to the small distances that their horse and wagons could take them. By 1922, there were 2.2 million automobiles on the nation's roads. With the help of Henry Ford and his assembly line, that number would increase to over 22 million by the end of the 1920s.

Society was also beginning to see a change in young women's behavior, exemplified by the "flapper";[3] and all were not pleased. In 1922, *The Pittsburgh Observer* noted, "a change for the worse during the past year in feminine dress, dancing, manners, and general moral standards," and warned against any "failure to realize the serious consequences in immodesty in girl's dress."

The 1922 *Farmer's Wife* Contest

The perception that city dwellers had of farm women in the 1920s was generally not favorable. It was commonly believed that the farm wife was a drudge and a slave, miserable with her life, and anxious—if not determined—to see her daughter escape from the farm when she was grown. *The Farmer's Wife*, a popular women's magazine of the day, with 750,000 subscribers, believed that this view was far from the truth.

In January 1922, the editors of the magazine asked their readers the following question: "If you had a daughter of marriageable age, would you, in the light of your own experience, want her to marry a farmer?"

The editors asked participants to "consider this question in all its angles. Talk it over with your husband, your children and your friends. Consider not only the financial side of the question but the moral and physical viewpoint and the things that make for real happiness. You wish the best things in the world for your children. Would your daughter as a farmer's wife be better off—all things considered—than she would be in the city or town?"

The magazine offered prizes for the best 68 answers submitted—$200 for first, $100 for second, $50 for third place, with an additional $150 to be divided among the remaining sixty-five winners.

By the end of the contest on March 1, 1922, the editors were overwhelmed with the response from over seven thousand readers. When the opinions were tallied, it was found that the editors were correct: 94 percent of farm wives stated that they would, indeed, want their daughter to marry a farmer.

A list of the winning entries is on page 250.

The Farmer's Wife **January 1922 magazine cover** ↔

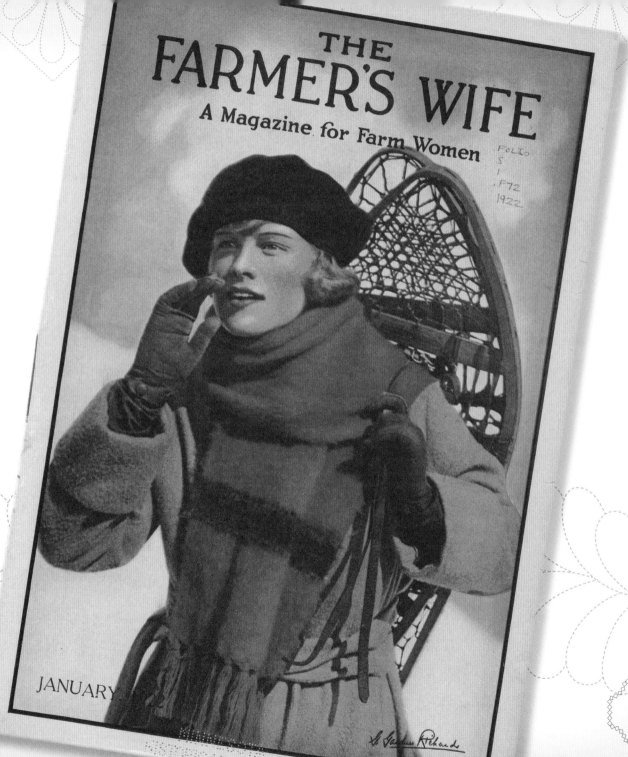

THE
FARMER'S WIFE
A Magazine for Farm Women

JANUARY

11

The Farm Wife Speaks

The editors of *The Farmer's Wife* compiled the letters from the sixty-eight contest winners into a small booklet entitled, "Do You Want Your Daughter To Marry A Farmer?" In the following pages, you will read excerpts from many of the winning letters.

While the focus of the letters was obviously not about the changing American culture, it is still interesting to note how rarely these changes were addressed by the farm women in 1922. Not one farm wife mentioned women's right to vote, prohibition, the radio, or changing standards in women's dress. Occasional references were made to vaudeville, jazz, moonshine, flappers and movies, but with few exceptions, they were not mentioned favorably.

It appeared that the farm women were thrilled with the popular inventions of the day that would make their lives easier: telephones, automobiles, lighting systems, running water, carpet sweepers and the like. Nonetheless, they wanted their family life and values to be left alone. These articulate, optimistic and visionary farm women of

1922 seemed quite content with their peaceful lives on the farm, spent with their husbands, children, neighbors, books and nature.

How to Use This Book

THE QUILT

I pieced my FARMER'S WIFE quilt by hand. Don't get me wrong. There is no superior merit in hand piecing. Nor is it any more "traditional" than machine piecing. In fact, beginning in the mid-nineteenth century, when the company Singer made home sewing machines affordable and widely available, hand-pieced quilts gave way to machine piecing. Notice the caption for the quilt on page 14, which credits hand piecing by the author and longarm machine quilting by Nell Coons. As you can see, I'm happy to mix the old with the new.

You will find general tips on assembling and finishing the quilt on pages 240-244. I made a queen-size quilt, 83" x 103", for this book. The fabric requirements, cutting instructions and quilt assembly diagrams for lap, twin, queen and king sizes are given on pages 245-248. Larger versions of the quilt assembly diagrams are provided on the CD-ROM.

THE BLOCKS

Each letter excerpt is accompanied by photos and simple illustrated instructions

for two pieced blocks from the FARMER'S WIFE quilt. The instructions for each block include an illustrated cutting list with numbers identifying the templates for making 6" x 6" blocks. You can print the templates from the CD-ROM that accompanies this book.

NOTES

Finally, as I read the contestants' letters, I had to research some of the things the writers referred to. The endnotes on page 251 include some of the research results I thought you might find interesting.

13

THE
Farmer's Wife
LETTER EXCERPTS & QUILT BLOCKS

↤ **The FARMER'S WIFE Quilt**
designed and hand-pieced by Laurie Aaron Hird
and longarm quilted by Nell Coons
83½" x 103"

Living in God's Open Air

Cut Glass Dish

If this question put by THE FARMER'S WIFE had been asked me fifty or even twenty years ago, I am sure I should have said No. But no position in life has changed so much this last fifty years, as the standing of the farmer's wife.

I could give you a hundred reasons for saying yes. I would have her marry a farmer because there she has the chance of living in God's open air, of living a pure life, away from the meanness of a rural town, and the petty things they make so much of and away from the temptations of a big town.

I would have my daughter bring of the very best to that farm home—the best of music, books, pretty clothes, dainty things for her house. I am speaking of the little things of life which really make up the most of it; big events only happen once in awhile.

I love the financial independence of the farm. To me a town wife seems to have a cramped life. She has to ask her husband for money. I earned mine, myself, by selling eggs, butter, cream, fresh vegetables and spring frys. Besides, I felt myself to be a helpmate in providing most things for the house while my husband paid off heavier bills and bought cattle. We always had the very best on our own table. I did not believe in taking it all to town. I did not feel that I had lost social standing by farm work; in fact, I thought more of myself for I felt I had beautified my labor.

How beautiful our home was! It was only of logs, covered in summer with a wild clematis vine. I told our doctor that after five o'clock on winter nights we became New York millionaires for we had our easy chairs, a big fireplace and good books. We could not have had more in a mansion.

Mrs. J. E. F.
Valley County, Mont.

Kitchen Woodbox

[54]

17

No Safer Road to Travel

Country Path

[24]

I know no safer road to travel through real living than my daughter would take if a farmer were her life companion. It matters not what kind of a farm nor where located nor does it make much difference what special part of farm life would be accented. It is the sense of safety, the assurance of food, shelter and drink, and the knowledge that work yields something definite, that gives happiness.

Reading matter? All you want and any kind, brought by the rural carriers. Music? Classics and comics, any and all kinds for Victrola[18] and other "players." Clothes? Ordered from a dozen catalogs and a world of pleasure in the ordering. Company? Over the telephone and also close connection, with any needed aid in the event of illness. Even the poorest little farm affords all this. Then the cellar full-stored, the fruits, vegetables and meats, fresh and cold-packed. There are church, Sunday school and day-school, all within the range for the trusty Ford. And there are picnics, camping trips, and the "going-to-see" more distant friends.

Work? Plenty of it and that is the best part. Work is not only health-giving but an absolute necessity to the well-being of all; and it is work like farming, that has visible results that give satisfaction.

Children? Of course. Nowhere else are [they] so welcome and on the farm they live and grow and develop like the flowers they are. Children love the God-made world and are hampered in any man-made one, no matter how gilded.

To wake up in the early morning to the bird calls, the animal greetings, is better than the best symphony concert ever played. To see the sun climb out of bed and reach out rosy fingers to pick up the dew drops from field and meadow, and to watch the joyous greeting of all nature, in the summer time, is worth more than silver and gold can buy.

 Mrs. E. M. L.
Furnas County, Neb.

Silver Lane

[79]

City Life Holds No Glamour

Flock

[34]

Having spent the first two years of my married life, as well as much of my childhood in Chicago, city life holds no glamour, no lure for me. I know *its* lacks too well. I would not exchange the homely joy of riding in a "tin Lizzie" in the country for the excitement of "keeping up with Lizzie" in the city or town. I have had more genuine enjoyment in caring for and breeding up my flock of beautiful White Rock chickens; more real pleasure in tending my flowers and vegetables, more honest satisfaction in working with the lambs and bees, than I ever experienced in the varied round of activities that made up my life in the city. Such wholesome, out-door work serves not merely as an absorbing occupation for the moment, a time-killer, so to speak but is also an investment which later pays well. There is not space here to tell of my love for the panorama of ever-changing beauty that unrolls from my cabin on the hilltop.

It must be admitted that country life has neither very many thrills nor frills, but it offers instead what is of more value to earnest men and women: wholesome living conditions, an excellent moral environment, opportunity for mental growth and spiritual development, and the possibilities of real and lasting happiness. It is my conviction that when America wearies of jazz and reverts, as a nation, to the ideals of her pioneer forefathers, many will find in the simple joys of the country an antidote to over-sophistication. We who are already on the land and love it, despite all its lacks, know the blessed peace and security and happiness that nature offers those who have discernment enough to "hold communion with her visible forms."

MRS. A. B. D.
Park County, Wyo.

Hill & Valley

[46]

Progress Is Our Watchword

Century of Progress

[18]

A farmer's wife does not put in long hours in the winter. This is when we have our good times, community parties, neighborly visits, shows once in a while. In the spring and fall we have long hours but we have no noisy whistles to wake us; the birds and the sun do that. We have the chance of filling our lungs with the purest early morning air and our stomachs with pure foods. And, if we feel like taking a holiday, we may. We have no time keeper, we are our own bosses and so we feel more like working because we are working for ourselves and can express our ideas if we want to.

The farmer's wife does not have a monotonous life. Every year, every season, every month, every week, every day, every hour she has something different to think of, so her mind ought not get rusty. Now that her city sister seems to pity the farmer's wife let all the farmers' wives straighten their backs, throw up their heads and shout, *"Don't pity me!* I am satisfied with my work because I have a chance to learn how I can do it best. I can get information from my state and county. My children's education is being better taken care of. My husband, through his Farm Bureau[2], can do his work better. We are no longer hayseeds. We are of some account now, so we are glad, glad, *glad* to work. We are interested in everything that's going to make farming better. Progress is our watchword, so watch out, for we're going on as fast as we can. This world must be made safe for the farmer's wife. Let's—start—now!"

MRS. L. C. F.
Montcalm County, Mich.

Hovering Birds

[51]

The Best of All Good Things

Mother's Dream

[58]

Wee daughter is having her nap and it's a good opportunity to tell you why I wish the best of all good things for our pride and hope and joy.

It is because I have known the happiness which comes of service, that I want my daughter to know it, too. Is there any greater joy, I wonder, than that of a hard task well done? When I have hurried with my work that I might do something extra outside, worked until I felt old and cross and tired, and the best man in all the world has said, "I certainly couldn't farm without you!" oh, how I've thrilled. It becomes a little song in my heart and lightens my work for days. And even if he weren't the best man, I think I could be quite happy with the thought: "I've earned my way today; I'm

helping with the most essential job on earth;
I'm working for a better future."

Then there's the beauty of family life on
the farm. Instead of seeing my son rushing off
with "the fellows," my daughter going off for a
good time that I'll know nothing about, and the
younger children coaxing to go to the movies,
we'll be spending our evening together with our
music, books or mutual friends, or going to
some amusement *together*. We don't have "sets"
on the farm, just "a set" that includes father,
mother and the children. Perhaps the young
folks plan the coasting parties, the straw-rides
and picnics but there's always a sprinkling of
older folks with young hearts and they aren't
in the way either.

CONTINUED ⇥

Seasons

25

Attic Windows

[1]

And last but not least, of the good things I desire for this daughter-o'-mine, are peace, a love of nature and time for quiet, happy thoughts. Can they be had by any other class of working people as easily as by the woman on the farm? She doesn't rush to finish her work that she may spend a day bargain-hunting—a day of hurry, worry and "me-first" thoughts; of spending money she shouldn't spend and gazing at things she wants and can't have. No; she may sit on the front porch a bit while she sews or mends or perhaps reads her most helpful magazine (to me that means

THE FARMER'S WIFE). She will see and feel and hear the beauty of the world—her world—and with an unruffled spirit she will go in and get supper for her hungry brood.

And so, folks, I want my daughter to marry a farmer, a good man, upright, steadfast and true, with visions of the farm-life-to-be in his heart. Then, hand and hand, they can work to make their dreams come true, and she will know the happiness I have known. I could not ask for more.

 MRS. S. O.
Mille Lacs County, Minn.

End of Day

[30]

I Love the Farm

Jackknife

[53]

I love the farm and I had rather be known as a farm woman than by any other name. I want to spend every bit of my strength and intelligence and every day of my life making farming more alluring. I find keenest zest in the fight that we farmers must make, if we are to secure the right future for our work.

I want my daughter to marry a farmer. I hope, if she is so fortunate, that he may be college or university trained. I hope he may regard Agriculture as man's divinest vocation, worthy of the thoughtful best effort of the highest intelligence. With my daughter as a real partner, I should wish him to work to make farming the most respected of professions and farm life happier.

I want my daughter to bear hardships more bravely, not to be relieved of them; to meet difficulties more sturdily; to face motherhood as the "heritage of the Lord." I want her to help build a home in which children may grow, who will some day carry on the ideals and continue the service that I shall have to leave unfinished.

Nothing ever compels so sweet and deep a response in a women's heart as does strength. I hope my daughter's husband, strong with the sun-browned strength of a farmer, clean-minded, true, may inspire in her the kind of love that will dare any obstacle. No ease that mere wealth could bring, no opportunity that fame or birth or prestige could bestow, could so develop in her the best of womanhood.

Cities have produced men whose work one must admire but think of the combination of strength and tenderness that can swing an ax or a corn-knife all day and, at night, bath a tiny baby and put it to sleep in its crib. Something too deep for expression or for tears, thrills at the thought! To give her an "easier time," should I deny my child? Let her know the tingle of nerves and brain and body stretched to the utmost in her fight for better ways upon the farm! Let her learn the joy of real work well done! Let her be a Farmer's Wife!

 Mrs. G. B. S.
Saline County, Mo.

Peace & Plenty

[64]

Worthwhile and Purposeful Things

Churn Dash

I lived the first twenty-one years of my life in a large city. The past twenty years have been spent on a large farm and my experiences have been such that I can truthfully say I would have my daughter marry a farmer.

While the city affords many forms of diversion, I have learned that true happiness is best found in doing real God-service. This the farm woman finds in raising fowls, making butter, curing meat, planting [a] garden, canning, drying and preserving. I find real joy in doing these worthwhile things that need to be done because the world needs the fruits of my labors. No joy born of city pleasures exceeds the joy I feel when my products flaunt the blue ribbon at the state fairs.

As a city woman I ran the gamut of formal teas and parties; as a farmer's wife I have done something of everything a farmer's wife has to do, and much that requires a man's strength.

An unbelievable metamorphosis has been wrought in my ideas and ways of living and I would not have it otherwise. There is something so good, solid and genuine about farm life, and so much of sham, veneer and hypocrisy about city life. Country life is a great developer of character, the farm woman accomplishes so many worthwhile, purposeful things and never ceases to grow in mind, character and soul.

I believe that a prerequisite of a woman's content, success and happiness on the farm is a broad education—college if possible. My education has been my chief asset on the farm. I began farm life by making a study of scientific farming, reading many agricultural magazines and government bulletins; the practical application of the knowledge gained brought me success and comforts and the enviable position of being somewhat of an authority upon farm-home matters, strange as this may seem.

CONTINUED

Squash Blossoms

[86]

Bowtie

[10]

My interest in all things rural, from the farm and farm home to schools and roads and politics, keeps me pleasantly and profitably employed in my leisure hours. By *working* when I work and by planning ahead I have leisure hours. The farm woman, even of very moderate means, by taking active interest in public affairs, becomes a leader and enjoys personal contact with some of the greatest men and women of our country; while the city woman of moderate means has few and limited pleasures and small chance of rising socially or publicly.

We farm women have been talked about, written about, surveyed and interviewed until it is a miracle we are not ruined. Never before has so much been done for any other class of people as our Government is doing for the farmer and his family. I myself feel most important and it tickles my vanity, buoys me up and keeps me feeling young and happy.

Whatever lacks there may be in my life on the farm, I can always find greater lacks in the city woman's life and I often make comparisons. When it comes to dress and style—we farm women love pretty and becoming clothes and like to appear correctly gowned. If each county could employ a sympathetic, woman adviser, who each season would meet the women at central points, bringing cuts of popular styles, samples, prices and helpful dress suggestions, I believe this would meet a real need. To us, other things come first and we neglect the study of clothes, consequently often appearing at a disadvantage. I long to be able to select proper and becoming apparel in a short time and without assistance but have not the time to make this a study.

Long life to my sister farm woman!

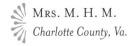 MRS. M. H. M.
Charlotte County, Va.

Ribbons

[74]

The Sense of Creation

Big Dipper

My daughter, married to a farmer, would be the real center of her home, the real partner of her husband—and each would be so happily busy in their little world that love triangles and divorce mills would have small chance at them. Result: serene hearts and minds which are the basis of deep physical strength and joy of living.

My daughter, married to a farmer, would not learn to depend on moving pictures and cheap shows for recreation. Her leisure (she really will have more than the city dweller might suppose) will be spent in delightful companionship with the good books and magazines her education will have taught her to appreciate.

The sense of creation, which makes her akin to God Himself, will be hers. Every spring she will witness and share in the age-old miracle—the new springing of hope, the delicious sensation of wondering what the earth will bring forth to establish the work of her hands; the knowledge that she, co-laborer with God, has helped to create something new, will bring a deep happiness and contentment that nothing else in this world can bring. When her heart can sing with the morning stars at the first stirrings of the new creation in spring and from that learn to go about her commonplace, homely tasks with still deeper joy over the faint fluttering of a new creation beneath her own heart, she will feel that heaven itself could not be a better place in which to live. Yes, I want my daughter to marry a farmer!

 Mrs. I. L. M.
Prince Georges County, Md.

Periwinkle

[66]

35

Better a Farmer ...

Night & Day

[59]

Why all this fuss about farmers' wives being slaves? Why select the wives of unkind or thoughtless husbands, and use them as examples of the farm women?

A large per cent of the farmers of today are broadminded, intelligent, progressive men. Many of the young men are college graduates who have learned to be gallant and considerate.

A farmer spends the winter months reading and has awakened to the fact that many farm wives are considered mere drudges. He thinks of what he has read, and applies it to himself. If he loves his wife, is she not in his thoughts? Is he not planning to make her life easier? Emphatically, yes!

Compare a farmer of moderate means with the common laboring man of the city. Does he have the means to give his wife many of the modern labor-saving devices? Does she attend afternoon teas and the best operas? No; from morning till night she toils, planning, saving, and trying to exist on his meager wage. Where can she go when mentally depressed? She hasn't the beautiful, wide out-doors, the green fields, flowers and trees, or the invigorating fresh air which the country woman has and loves. She only has that stuffy, little house and if she steps outside, she is on the street, surrounded by noise, walls and people. Does not the farmer's wife who is striving to make a home with a few dollars, have an untold advantage over this city wife?

Would I want a daughter of mine to marry a farmer? Yes, indeed! If she chooses a poor man, better a farmer than a common laborer. If a wealthy man is to be her choice, why not have a beautiful country home?

Mrs. C. R. M.
Ramsey County, N.D.

Tall Pine Tree

[94]

37

Farmer's Daughter/Farmer's Wife

Cats & Mice

[17]

Looking back over the years that I have been a farmer's daughter and a farmer's wife, I have no hesitancy in saying that I wish my daughter to marry a farmer. Financially, the farm woman has her pay envelope every week in the butter and egg money, and she is a poor financier, indeed, who cannot squeeze from the grocery list a little for her own private use; the joy of spending is not marred by the thought that she has not earned it. With a well-filled cellar of all kinds of fruits and vegetables, a year's supply of lard and meat, there is no danger of starvation. Let the world go mad as it will, she is independent in that respect, as well as in a financial way.

From a physical standpoint, nothing can be more invigorating than the daily exercise in the open air, the routine of tasks that are always full of interest, the joy of accomplishment of things worthwhile. The farm is teaming [*sic*] with life of all kinds, from new-born calves to downy chicks. While a Rubens[II] is pottering about in a stuffy studio, striving to reproduce on canvas a small portion of the beauty and the color that he sees around him, a farm woman will be engaged in producing all this that is so pleasing to the eye and which can never be copied in its entirely. Does a Rosa Bonheur[I] gain fame by painting animals? My daughter will raise those animals and bring them to a perfection which her paintings can never hope to attain, all the while surrounded by God's sweet and wholesome air and the beauty of His world.

MRS. C. B. H.
Clay County, Miss.

Windblown Square

[107]

39

An Orchard in Bloom

Maple Leaf

I f a farmer's daughter is not happy as a farmer's wife, I don't know who could be. Of course there is work. Yes, lot's of it! Farm life can never be run on an eight-hour schedule, any more than motherhood can, for we are dealing too closely with nature. But it certainly has its compensations. To be sure, I might not enjoy farm life so much if my husband treated me as though I could not understand finance or figures, as I've heard of some men doing. My husband and I are partners in everything. I keep the books of the company. I do not ask him for money any more than he asks me. We talk over our prospects and expenditures together. I don't think it is practical for a farmer's wife to have an allowance, because his income is so uncertain. If she is a partner, she can spend intelligently.

Can you think of anything in city life that compares with an orchard in bloom? I haven't time to sit down and *gaze* very often, but just a glance out of doors now and then while I'm about my work, makes me feel all chirpy inside, like a robin sounds! On our limited income, in the city, we'd have to take our outings in a park but here we have more houseroom than we know what to do with and park scenery to enjoy as far as we can see.

 Mrs. G. W. N.
Ingham County, Mich.

Practical Orchard

[69]

41

The Very Breath of Life

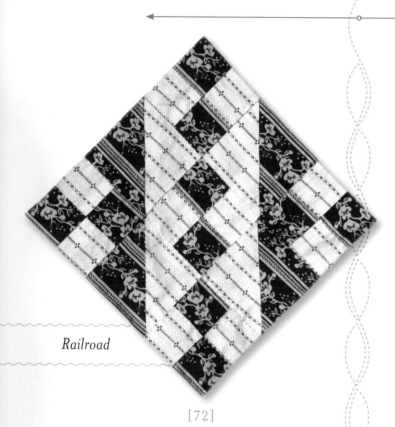

Railroad

This is a question which all of us, who have daughters, should regard with all seriousness. As we are asked to answer it by the *light of our own experience*, I would say that I was a town girl but I married a farmer to whom the country is the very breath of life. I have only to close my eyes and again in memory come back those first *lonely years*. The long solitary days when for hours no sound broke the silence, save the hum of bees, the song of a bird, or the low of the cattle. Yet to me, with the blood of town bred in my very bones—to whom the sound of a locomotive, the tread of passing feet, was music—to me, in all these years, has come a love of country which surpasses all.

There have been many changes in country life in the last few years. The women's work is no longer the so-called drudgery pictured by many (though if we love our work it should never be that to us). The country has now so many advantages copied from the city—telephones, electricity, running water, furnaces, autos, and so forth. Few are the farmers who do not have some or all of these conveniences. I believe that farmers, as a class, have only just begun to realize some of the good things that the future has in store for them.

The country is no longer the solitary place of ten years ago. The motor-horn is heard in the quietest places and the noise of machinery is on every hand. The distance from country to city is reduced to a minimum by the automobile. The best of the city—its concerts, lectures, churches, and the newest of books and magazines, are within reach of all.

 Mrs. F. W. C.
Chautauqua County, N.Y.

Wrench

[111]

43

'Round the Circle

Four Winds

[38]

Out of my first haste I said in answer to the *The Farmer's Wife* question "it all depends on the farmer." Then I noticed that you ask "out of your experience" and then I said Yes for in no other life would the comradeship of these twenty years have been possible.

Experience—well, in that I have been about 'round the circle. There was no one to help us to a start. We rented the first year on share, everything furnished. The next year we lived on a quarter-section homestead of buffalo grass, thirty-five miles from town. I helped build the one-room, unplastered, 12 x 14 shack. And there was a baby, too. Then we went "back East" as renters again. After a while there was a deed to a run-down, heavily mortgaged farm.

I have done all the usual things—chickens, garden, canning, cooking for hired men and so forth. I have also milked, picked corn, shocked grain and run nearly every machine used on a Western farm. We have dried out, drowned out, hailed out and burnt out. Always we drew together, looked in each other's eyes and whispered "Tough! But we have each other and the children. We'll make it."

Now on a half section, hardwood finished, furnace heated, electric powered and lighted house, the homestead baby away at school, others in the grades, I say Yes to your question.

CONTINUED ➝

Weathervane

[100]

45

Corn & Beans

[22]

Lonely and isolated farm! Heavens! Sometimes I've almost prayed for a blizzard or a quarantine. I never lived closer than ten miles to town and once I was there only twice in two years. But we have boosted every neighborhood activity, entertained and arranged for bishops, missionaries and lecturers. In the little houses we did not use our one bedroom often enough to get acquainted with it but how well we knew the ridge down the middle of a sanitary cot!

For my children I covet happiness, development and service and that they may "live in a house by the side of the road." Happiness is not a matter of locality but of training and congenial companionship.

Twelve miles from town, this neighborhood has no excuse for arrested development. The W. C. T. U.[19] furnishes citizenship, domestic science and child-welfare classes; oratorical, essay, musical and poster contests, programs on the hundred and one other interests of this amazingly diversified organization. There were home nursing and botany classes. Then there's the State circulating library, the individual loan library, extension services offered in both study course and lectures for the state colleges. Where can my daughter better develop mentally or spiritually or find larger opportunity to serve?

And if she should be poor? Hoeing in the sun, dipping for chicken lice or milking in fly time are better than washing for strangers in a dark, ugly part of a city with children always underfoot, saving heat, saving light and eating cheap food. I'd rather she had corn cob heat and real food even if she had to produce it.

If there are fair circumstances, there is no law to compel her to work herself to death anywhere. Let him be a farmer if he be the right kind of man.

 MRS. W. R.
Hutchinson County, S.D.

W.C.T.U.

[99]

47

Well-Balanced and Happily Busy

Contrary Wife

[21]

There are two types of folk in this world who "muss up my disposition," to an absurd degree and I'm not sure which is the more obnoxious to me but in point of numbers, I think the people rank first who admit that life on the farm "is all right for a few weeks in the summer, when you can have all the fried chicken you want, for nothing; and it *might* be all right all the year 'round, if you had all the comforts of the city."

Close upon the heels of these come crowding those others who pity us because of our loneliness and who recite ghastly statistics concerning farm women who have lost their minds because of this loneliness.

Let me tell you that the woman who can't keep her mind well-balanced and happily busy, on a farm, would probably be an entirely useless member of society, no matter where she lived. Of all places and occupations, the farm and its work are the most fascinating.

To the women who harp and prattle about "all the conveniences of the city," I'd like to remark that a goodly number of women who live in the cities do not have all the afore-mentioned conveniences; and if the family is capable of earning enough, in the city, to provide them, they'd probably have them on the farm. In other words, the farm woman who does not have modern conveniences, would probably have to do without them if she moved to the city.

Unless my daughters love and are loved by men whose business makes it impossible for them to live on a farm, I hope they will marry farmers.

CONTINUED

Flower Basket

[35]

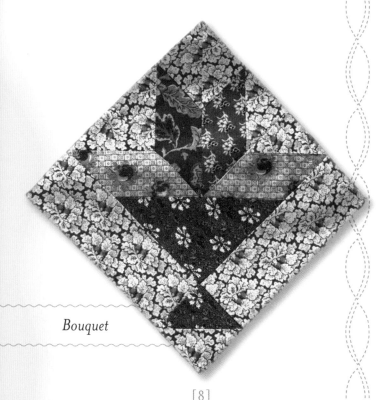

Bouquet

[8]

We live in one of those much-talked-about homes where folks do *not* have all the modern conveniences but we *do* have good books, good music and a wealth of flowers and growing things about us. Above all else, we live *together*, working and playing and planning together, as families must do, if the love and unity of that family are to become an inspiration to its members and to the community in which they live.

Our family doesn't depend upon the corner grocery for food or the pool room, the dance hall, or the movies for entertainment. We're not very likely to have any great moral problems on our hands, as the children grow up, and we shan't depend upon a social worker or a soap-box orator to save them from sin and poverty.

Our children are learning to be self-supporting, self-respecting citizens, and they're doing it under the guidance of a father and mother whose lives are consecrated to that very task and through that task, to the service of humanity.

We know, because we have tried it, that our family life could never have been kept so intact, nor our happiness so secure, if we had lived any place other than on the farm.

And we can ask for no greater happiness for a child of ours, than that he may have a home like ours, and that our happiness and our home ideals may live on, in their children and their children's children.

C. Mc. D. B.
Marion County, Ind.

Peaceful Hours

[65]

A Wonderful Gift

Country Farm

[23]

Having lived in both city and country, I feel that I can discuss with fairness, the advantages of country life from the woman's viewpoint and as one of the working class.

We farm women of today need no pity. We have as many conveniences and pleasures as city women and we make use of our opportunities. Of course we have a great deal of work but we are fully repaid by the satisfaction of knowing that we are of real use in the great game of life.

Do not imagine that our time is spent trudging from the spring with a pail of water, doing chores, or confining ourselves to a dreary, ugly kitchen gazing with longing eye to the world beyond. Those are versions of farm life twenty years ago. Very few women do outside work, with the exception of caring for the chickens.

With the improved roads we easily reach the city 15 or 30 miles away to shop, attend lecture, concert or movie. Our chauffeur doesn't drive us in, we "flivver"[4] it ourselves!

Nearly 80% of Wisconsin farmers own automobiles. The following facts taken from a farm survey in our county in 1921 will help to show that we are not so far behind the times:

Number of farm homes	3,460
Number of automobiles.............	2,500
Number of oil, gas, or electric stoves	1,925
Number of pianos or Victrolas[18] ...	2,120
Number of power washers...........	1,300
Number of farms having running water in the house	1,260

Can the working class of the city show a better record?

CONTINUED

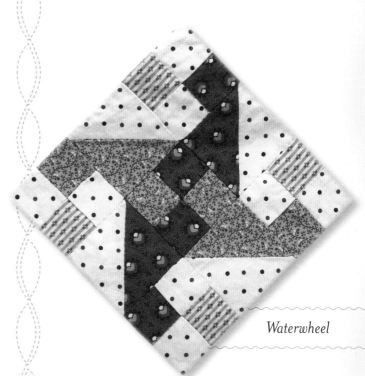

Waterwheel

[98]

53

Northern Lights

[61]

A Wonderful Gift, CONTINUED

Perhaps our husbands are not able to spare the money for luxuries or conveniences we wish. We are always able to make extra money from our chickens. And we have learned what a great many steps and discomfort can be saved in our work.

We do admit that we have a lack of amusements but the lack may be a blessing. There are thousands of city hearts sick with misery caused by over-abundance of amusements.

In late years our schools have become as efficient as city schools. In one respect even better. Hot lunches are served to the youngsters. With pure air, good food and plenty of exercise, they develop into strong men and women.

In farm homes each child is taught daily to perform some tasks and be responsible for their being well done; this fits him to perform capably the serious tasks of later life. Too few

54

city children are taught to be industrious at a time when the habit of industry ought to be formed.

Last but not least, of all the restless world, we, from the beauty and tranquility of the country, the knowledge of our use to the world and our independence, have in our souls the peace and content that money cannot purchase. That surely is a wonderful gift.

"They lived happily ever after." So end the fairy tales the children love. If fairies still ruled the world, would that they might grant that my daughter, the Princess, wed the Prince of the Soil, and live happily ever after in God's country, land of sunshine and flowers, health and happiness.

 MRS. I. G.
Sauk County, Wis.

Single Wedding Star

[80]

55

Militia of Arguments

Honey's Choice

[50]

Yes! And am pleased to muster out my militia of arguments. I hope to trounce the opposition with [eight] shots.

Shot One. Farms are safe investments; the ever-increasing value of land is more than the offsetting depreciation. In the city, my daughter and her family are at the mercy of recurrent panics.

Two. For private enterprise and experiment, the farm is without parallel. Above general grain-and-stock-farming, there are specialties such as ginseng, mushrooms, loganberries, honey. Even weeds and stones may be tangible assets.

Three. Many rural families enjoy electric light, plumbing, automobiles and *all* rural families may enjoy unobstructed sunlight, blossoming trees, stimulating breezes—perhaps also the daily newspaper.

Four. On the farm, my daughter and her family can have fresh air, fresh milk, eggs and butter without looking into the pocketbook.

Five. Daily exertion means bodily strength and varied responsibilities favor moral caliber.

Six. On the farm, you are quite independent of fads and fashions. Cotton stockings, sun-bonnets, bloomers and overalls are all right, and you feel happier than the walking fashion-plate.

Seven. As a farmer's wife, my daughter is a teacher and a business woman, as well as a mother and wife. She rules over the egg, fruit and poultry department, not always for the sake of pin-money, but for the sake of helping her partner peel off "the plaster" on their property. Her city sister, unless strong enough to be her husband's treasurer, may have to wheedle and beg.

Eight. On the farm my daughter's husband and her growing boys are more aloof from vicious allurements. Instead of vaudeville and moonshine, they have the box-social and friendly games of skat[14]. Vamping[16] is very uncommon, and the necessity of birth control is not so apparent.

E. S.
Milwaukee County, Wis.

Temperance Tree

[95]

The Threads of Life

Spider Web

[83]

Yes, I want both my daughters to marry farmers.

I was born on this farm and excepting the first eight of the twenty years of my married life, I have resided here. Perhaps the broader vision I gained of city life during those eight years, is responsible for my decision.

My husband and I lived the comfortable lives of the great, middle-class. My time was filled with my babies, friends and the wonders of our National Capital. I was happy but for one thing, our lack of family life, caused by my husband's long office hours. I well remember the time our baby cried with fright when his father, who idolized him, picked him up. Surely, a system that placed the home-making and child training on one parent alone, permitting even a temporary estrangement of father and child, was wrong.

Circumstances made it necessary for us to return to the farm. We took up the threads of life again, in the old homestead—which, though homey and substantial, lacked all the improvements of our recent modern home. But the birds sang, the flowers blossomed everywhere and the trees whispered their soothing secrets. Was I not as wealthy in these possessions as I had been in modern fixtures?

CONTINUED ↦

Wild Goose Chase

[105]

Farmer's Daughter

[32]

And my girls! They reveled in the outdoor life. The elder understood, naturally, the "still, small voice that comes from earth and her waters and the depths of air." Her younger sister unconsciously absorbed until the sunshine crept into her heart and came forth a disposition of rare sweetness. It was her hands that helped the lame baby chick or hurt birdie and I knew that some day her understanding of service would mean to alleviate the suffering of humanity. Thus my girls grew, with God's wonderful outdoors and dominant influence, until, at budding womanhood, they are as genuine and wholesome as the color in their cheeks, and too busy with the real things of life, and with their education, to be frivolous or superficial or artificial, as are so many modern girls.

As I look at them, I realize that motherhood is the greatest, the biggest and the holiest thing any woman may experience; and I firmly believe that should motherhood be theirs, they will be better prepared physically, mentally and spiritually because of their rural environment, which I consider has been their parents' greatest help in character building. And I desire that they receive like aid in the rearing of their families.

Mrs. G. R. B.
Wood County, W. Va.

Fruit Basket

[42]

Country Home Life

Friendship

[39]

*Y*es. I have two young daughters, although not yet of marriageable age but I wish them both to marry farmers. First, because the country home life is more nearly complete in itself, and therefore productive of real happiness. Each member has important duties which make him necessary to the whole. The city draws from the home, not toward it.

The school or community hall is usually the place for social gatherings which are made a success though the efforts of all the members of the family. While the city family goes to the movies or other place of amusement and pays to be entertained, the rural family is probably engaged in taking part in the program which is staged twice a month at the community hall.

Father and mother may have parts in the small play; young people debate, little folks recite or are active in their club work. This develops leadership in many. Community singing will be a great help in the near future. Instead of going to the restaurant after the show, as in the city, the group which, in its turn, furnishes refreshments, serves a delicious lunch of wholesome food, after the program. In our community almost every family—including every member thereof—attends Sunday School each Sunday and church service when it is held, which is about once a month at present.

Mrs. J. J. T.
Cascade County, Mont.

Square Dance

[85]

Independence and Charm

Darting Birds

[27]

There is a wholesomeness about farm life, an independence and charm not found in any other industry. There is spring time, blossom time, fruit time, harvest time and the long winter evenings by the fireside. There's a flower for every month of the year.

The wife of the successful farmer must rise early and is usually the last to retire but all the hours from dawn till bedtime are not necessarily full of work.

The average farmer's wife who plans her work can find a number of hours for reading, writing and social pleasures and in this day of autos and good roads, has time and opportunity for movies, concerts and lectures. The woman who is a drudge on a farm will be a drudge wherever you put her. It is lack of management, lack or order and lack of backbone and brains that make drudgery.

The country is a clean, natural place to rear children; there is an abundance of fresh air and wholesome food; we keep more natural hours; and by the time the children are ready for higher education, good habits, good health and clean morals are already assured.

So, I want my daughter to marry a farmer and I want to see her in her own home on a good American farm with the cleanness and wholesomeness of country life lived close to nature, in daily intercourse with flowers and birds and bees, chickens, and cows and pigs, horses and autos and tractors, pianos, Victrolas[18] and telephones, with all the joys and pleasures of an American home in God's wonderful out-of-doors.

Mrs. R. C. W.
Jasper County, Mo.

Hovering Hawks

[52]

Live a Successful Life

Duck & Ducklings

[28]

"The tilling of the soil is the most healthful, the most useful and the most noble occupation of man."

—GEORGE WASHINGTON

Could there be a better reason than that expressed in these words of Washington for wanting my daughter to marry a farmer? What other position requires the knowledge and skill as does that of the farmer's wife? She must be a home-maker, that is, she must be skilled in cooking, sewing, washing, ironing, making beds, setting tables, sweeping, dusting, cleaning, buying, nursing, educating the children, as well as social manager and anything else her hand finds to do indoors.

Then outside she must be a livestock breeder, that is, raise chickens, turkeys and so forth. If her husband is a stock farmer, she must learn pedigrees and keep records of them. She must be a gardener, know how to can, preserve and store her fruits and vegetables, how to care for her meat in winter, how to make soap and many other things. What other position in life requires as much knowledge and skill as to be a farmer's wife? Nor is she a drudge because she performs these many tasks; she is a financier, a bookkeeper, and home-maker, a manufacturer, a canner, a trained nurse, a teacher and a livestock breeder. She is a real business woman.

CONTINUED

Star Gardener

[87]

Evening Star

[31]

The so-called privileges of city life are few in comparison to the contentment and love for nature that we enjoy in the country. We learn to care for and feed the living things. In the country we have beautiful views. From our farm I can see a stretch of miles and miles of God's beautiful country. Men have deeds to land, but the beautiful view they do not own. That belongs to all the country people. How can we help but thank God that we can live in the beautiful country! Even night in the country with its stars and its dews is a wonderful blessing when compared to the life of people who are shut between walls and behind curtains.

What is success for a woman but home? And where could you find [a] better environment for a home than on the farm? Why should I want my daughter to leave these beautiful surroundings where home can be made a paradise and the woman a wonderful home-maker? The memory of the farm home will be treasured long, long after the screen artist has married and divorced her fourth husband, or been murdered, or the stenographer has discovered that he who is false to one can be the same with two, and money doesn't buy happiness. Home endures. So I want my girl to marry a farmer that she may have the best chance to live a successful life and of being a real home-maker.

 MRS. R. A. S.
Shawnee County, Kan.

Homemaker

[47]

The Brightest and Happiest Place on Earth

Flower Pot

[37]

Home economics have been put within the reach of every farm girl, so that even though a mother may be a poor cook or an indifferent housekeeper, her daughter need not be. The teaching of home economics in our rural schools has dignified housekeeping so the young woman of today is not ashamed of her vocation and does not care to go to town to take up office work or clerking. These home-economic courses include cooking, baking, canning, preserving and general household management.

The farm home of today is far different from what it used to be and the daughter is not ashamed to have her friends visit her as used to be the case. The farm home has or can have the some conveniences, comforts and beautiful surroundings that are possible in the homes in the city, and house work does not mean the drudgery that it has meant. The young people are learning that farming is a respectable and profitable business viewed from a practical, business standpoint, and that both the farmer and the farmer's wife can take more pride in building up a real farm home, which included conveniences for the farmer in good buildings, good fences, purebred stock and up-to-date machinery and, for the wife, a well-arranged house with the various labor-saving devices such as oiled floors, carpet sweeper, built-in features, lighting and water systems, steam pressure cooker and so forth, than they could possibly take in building up a home in the city.

Therefore rural life, with its independence, its beauties, its culture and its improvement, make the farmer's home the brightest and happiest place on earth.

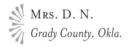 Mrs. D. N.
Grady County, Okla.

Garden Path

[43]

Partners

Broken Dishes

B orn on a farm, I hated everything pertaining to farm life as I knew it as a child. I met a young farmer with high ideals and deserted a promising musical future to marry him. And now, do I want my daughter to marry a farmer? Why not,—when that would insure our grandchildren a splendid physical development?—one hundred sixty acres on which to romp and play, without the neighbors yelling, "keep off the grass!" Besides the animal pets which all farm children have, our community boasts several homes where basketball and tennis courts have been erected for the neighborhood children's use.

Husband and wife need to come to an understanding, the first thing, that she needs new modern implements as well as he. Also the "chore" question should be settled early in the action.

I have never milked a cow. Why? Because I told my husband I wouldn't and he doesn't expect it. I count my hands more valuable to me as a pianist than as a milk maid. My husband and I are partners in this farming business but we each respect the other's rights.

Some farmers think they have to work all day and half the night. My husband plans his work so that his chores are all done at dark or before, and the evening is spent with his family, singing and playing, or possibly visiting with a neighbor. In that way I get the supper dishes washed before midnight, too.

When Gluck[7] or Galli-Curci[6], Sousa[15] or Kreisler[10] or other geniuses come to the nearest city, we drive in and hear them, but those who are unable to do this, by means of phonographs can bring these treats to their homes. Good literature and good music mean so much to any home.

 MRS. J. R. F.
Canadian County, Okla.

Checkerboard

[19]

True to Her Higher Ideas

Tulip

[96]

There is more and harder work for the housewife on the farm than in town, but in a well-ordered farm home it is done under conditions that contribute to her physical development. The most perfect specimens of womanhood are found on the farm; the mother who has borne and reared a large family under good conditions and with the exercise of intelligent management is the best preserved, most cheerful and beloved of them all.

She who is true to her higher ideals will find time for unselfish community service. There are many tactful, soul-cheering things the country wife can do for others by which her own life is enriched.

There are few divorces in the country, few crimes committed or homes disgraced. The idea of luxury is modest and the large fortune is the exception.

I sometimes read morbid articles on the monotony of farm life! I am thankful at such times for a well-developed sense of humor;

I smile, and to rest my eyes, look long into the shadows of the dark evergreens close beside the window and think of the many new interests of farm life, from the new baby, either our own or our neighbor's, to the first brood of downy chicks; the tiny pigs; the new calf and colt and lambs; the tender green rows across the garden; the long brown furrows beyond; the wheat field's new glory; the first tulips and jonquils; the blossoming bough; delicate green verdure; the flash of the blue bird's wing and the oriole's return to the maple where various other birds, a family of squirrels and a pair of little owls find homes, rent free.

I want my daughter to marry a farmer that they may live where God speaks to them through nature and where their minds may have the ever-present uplift that glorifies toil and adds dignity to the humblest duty.

 M. P. E.
Nodaway County, Mo.

Pine Tree

[67]

75

I Lost My Heart to a Farmer

Broken Sugar Bowl

[12]

I have lived twenty years in the country and seventeen in a large city (Boston), so know both lives well. A few years ago, I should have cried out with all my powers, "No! Never shall daughter of mine be a farmer's wife." Raised in the country, I determined young never to stay there. I pursued an education through college, became well established in a large city, and then, lo, I lost my heart to a farmer! But I acquired no love for the farm and settling in a district inhabited by the old-fashioned farmer and wife, I soon despised everything connected with farm life—except my husband. Because I so loved him and he so loved farming, I decided to see what could be done to relieve the situation. I tabulated the pros and cons:

PROS

1. Husband interested and contented.
2. Independence, and so many hours together.
3. Higher moral tone than city life.
4. Abundance of room and fresh air.
5. Fresh eggs, milk and vegetables.

CONS

1. Mud.
2. Inconveniences.
3. Lack of money.
4. Lack of water.
5. Lack of society.
6. Lack of beauty.
7. Monotony of diet.
8. Monotony of thought.
9. Untidyness of everything.
10. "Early to bed, early to rise."

CONTINUED

Farmer's Puzzle

[33]

77

Grape Basket

The "cons" so intruded themselves that I couldn't appreciate the "pros" and hubby and I determined to tackle those "cons" with all our brain and brawn, for he made me see that with them removed, farming would be *THE life*.

Ditching, draining and cinder-paths helped No. 1 [mud].

It will be years before we have No. 2 [inconveniences] eradicated in reality, as we have on paper; but a definite plan is a big help and each convenience we complete is a joy realized after much pleasant anticipation. We chose hens, cream, asparagus and fruit as side lines to give some monthly income to supplement the main crops. These not only added to our pocketbook but gave variety to our diet, both fresh and canned. I also planned greater variety of vegetables, and lengthen the season by use of a hotbed.

Side by side, we planned the beautiful and practical, and some day our home will be truly elegant.

I bought an oil stove and fireless cooker. I get the breakfast at night, except what Hubby can quickly finish on oil stove, and so I get up early only on special occasions and ask him to sit up late only on special occasions.

Magazines and a telephone make me part of the world and I try to keep abreast of the times. We are the happiest couple I know, have more chance to enjoy each other on a farm than elsewhere and I can wish no greater blessing for my daughter than the love of a farmer like "Dad."

 Mrs. G. R. E.
Morgan County, Ala.

Morning

[57]

Clear-Eyed and Clear-Hearted

Box

[9]

I realize what it might mean to my daughter to marry a farmer. I habitually do all the housework for eight people, make cottage cheese and butter to sell and do all the family sewing. Not habitually, but as circumstances have made it necessary, I have carried water, led horses for ploughing and planting, raked hay, picked and husked field corn and dug potatoes. Yet I find, take or make time to read and keep somewhat in touch with current events. I also am interested in dietetics, child-welfare books or magazines articles, good farm magazines, and, for recreation, books by good authors, poets and playwrights. I probably read about eighty books per year, besides magazines.

Not because of the long hours and hard work, for I agree with Sir Clifford Sifton[13] that these are to be counted as draw-backs, but in *spite* of these and because of the purity of thought and depth of understanding gained by the comparative isolation of farm life, I most emphatically would wish my daughters to marry farmers.

CONTINUED +—>

Prairie Queen

[70]

Birds in the Air

[7]

Where, except on the farm, can you find the close companionship, the common interests, the congeniality of such a perfect understanding of each other's daily work, ambitions and successes, as there is between husband and wife on the farm? Where, except on the farm, can you find a place where parents can teach their children the lessons of truth and right living, without being constantly overshadowed by the rough, uncouth language of outsiders or the sometimes unspeakable things taught by older playmates?

The farmer cares for many forms of farm life from their earliest infancy to full maturity. Can he do so and not learn of God's wonderful care and tenderness for all to which He gives form? Can we watch over the tiny seedling, the wobbly calf, the toddling baby feet, and not gain in our own souls some of God's tenderness?

It seems to me that a farmer usually has what it pleases me to call "vision." Months and years of daily association with nature uplifts him, gives him a vivid idea of God in nature and brings him nearer to what God meant His people to be. What is there in cities that can give a man or woman this ever-widening vision of the meaning of life?

When someone offers my daughter love, marriage and a home, I would much rather it would be a clear-eyed, clean-hearted, penniless farmer than a city man with a white-collar position and a large salary.

Mrs. C. M. B.
Cheshire County, N.H.

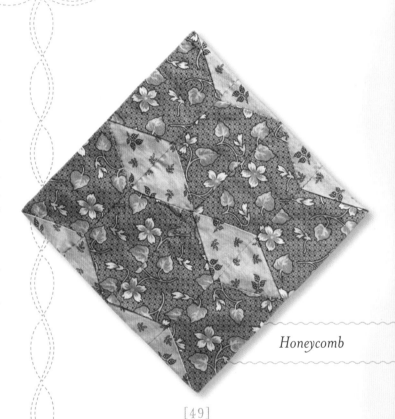

Honeycomb

[49]

The Lure of Mother Earth

Cups & Saucers

At the outset, one must refute the current false statements regarding a woman's life on the farm, namely: "no modern improvements!" and "too isolated!" They are in a class with the bogy man and similar imaginary terrors.

Thanks to one-pipe furnaces, farm lighting systems, septic tanks and the expert knowledge of rural sanitation disseminated by farm papers and Government bulletins, a farm can have modern improvements—even a pre-Revolutionary farmhouse, like this of mine.

That other bugbear, isolation, can be answered in the key of "F", as it were—Flivvers[4], Fones and Free Rural Delivery[5].

Do you realize, girls, that when you marry a farmer your husband is your own? Think: that matrimony may mean for you entering into the one business partnership possible for a husband and wife wherein the woman may still be mother and home-maker.

Ponder upon the fact, Mothers, that the bright daughter, who might be a nobody in a large city, can be a real power in a small farm community, working for and through the rural organizations, the school, the library, the church and her children. It is upon the farm that her mind may be kept broad and alert by much reading, much thinking; her heart kept sympathetic and warm by communion with God's out-of-doors: her spirit kept from being tarnished by vamping[16] and jazz; and her feet kept on the ground.

There certainly is an abundance of honest toil on a farm, but how about the hard work involved in "keeping up with the Joneses?" Can any self-respecting woman doubt which labor is more important?

We must keep in mind the fundamentals of existence: the vital worth of food, the importance of shelter, the value of effort. Who wouldn't be a pilgrim, a pioneer? To fare forth with your good man to wrestle with primitive things, to thrill throughout your being at the lure of Mother Earth? The farm today offers you your one chance for such a great adventure.

 E. M. W.
Dukes County, Mass.

Postage Stamp

[68]

Satisfaction of Being a Real Helper

Rainbow Flowers

[73]

Farming is the only business which a woman automatically can enter, upon marriage, as her husband's assistant manager. This gives her an importance beyond that of being merely a wife, and a mother of his children, dependent for a livelihood upon industrial conditions, or upon his ability to please his employer. Without her services the garden, poultry and dairy would bring them little profit. Having these products, living is assured, and beyond this, is the satisfaction of being a real help-meet.

The mind of a farmer's wife is continually broadening by the variety of her interests. Bees, berries, babies; cheese, chicks, canning; grub, garments, garden—do these suggest an empty mind? How can her life be monotonous?

She spends the greater part of her day doing constructive work. Unusual, indeed, must be the mind which fails to find among these duties, one in which to place an absorbing interest. Outside of the city's confusion there is a chance to express one's best and deepest self in that work. Ruskin[12] says, "When we are rightly occupied, our amusement grows out of our work as the color-petals out of a fruitful flower." Feeling this, my daughter never will grow indifferent to the results of what she is doing. Her heart will sing the song of Van Dyke[17]:

"This is my work. My blessing, not my doom,
Of all who live, I am the one by whom it can be done
in the right way."

CONTINUED ⇥

Strawberry Basket

[91]

Buzzard's Roost

[15]

I want my grandchildren to have the best of diet—milk, vegetables, fruits—and plenty of room to play. I want them to know the recreation that comes from associating with growing things and with the season's changes. I want their taste in art, music and books to be developed from the home atmosphere. And I ask, above all things, that in order to develop the poise so necessary in carrying out a fixed purpose for her children, she be located safely away from the dictates of a world always eager to overrule a mother's authority.

I am not dismayed by the fact that in my own experience my reading has been curtailed, and my vacations few in number. I predict for my daughter no such life of servitude as ours has been. Our education did not fit us for our work. Looking into the future, I see her forming permanent friendships with boys and girls having tastes and aspirations similar to her own. Team work in school activities prepares them for pooling their individual interests in community enterprises, such as a community laundry, sewing room, canning kitchen, power plant and water system. As the co-operative spirit lifts the burden of heavy tasks, so the centralized social life eliminates the isolation of country living. A wave of pride sweeps over me as I see the barren country blossoming like the rose under their capable management: drudgery over, poverty ended, feuds all past. Rising with the birds and sharing in their songs, their happy hearts proclaim, "We are American farmers' wives; queens, creators, rulers, lovers, among mankind!"

Mrs. G. B. H.
Richland County, Mont.

Rosebud

[75]

High Lights and Shadows

Linoleum

[55]

I have lived on the farm and in the city. I have found high lights and shadows in each. Life on the farm is not the simple combination of fresh air, flower gardens, butter and eggs that some city sisters envy us for, and yet—I would have my two daughters marry farmers because I think they will be most likely to find there the three conditions that make for a married woman's happiness.

First, she and her husband must be real partners. Nowhere is there a better chance for this than on the farm. There, John does not kiss Mary goodbye in the morning, and leave her a widow until business releases him in the evening. They plan the day together.

John tells what work he has in mind, and Mary mentions the coming incubator hatch or the possibility of setting out cabbages. At a pinch, Mary may ride the plow or run the tractor but always they know that both are working for what both spend. It is not John's salary, but John and Mary's income.

Second, a woman must have a reasonable number of working conveniences. Just as I have linoleum, a power washer, a telephone and other conveniences my mother did not start out with, so I may reasonably hope that my daughters will have electric power, running water and other conveniences that city house-keepers have.

CONTINUED ·|·→

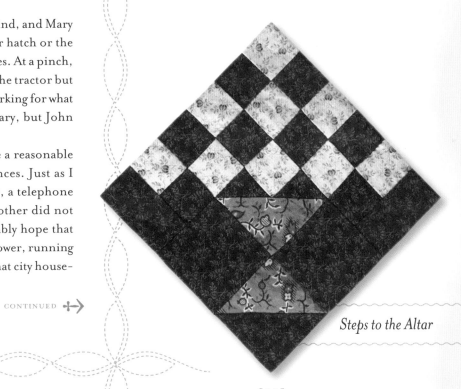

Steps to the Altar

Puss in the Corner

[71]

Third, and not least, her children must have the best possible chance. I have seen children playing on the city dumping ground, fighting in the alley, or daring the street cars to run them down. I have seen them also in comfortable home yards and city playgrounds but, after all, God made the country for the child. A yard isn't enough. He needs a pasture, a field, a piece of woods, a stream of water and pets.

I began my education in an old-time school with all the old-time drawbacks. My children attend a graded school in town. They have sand tables and busy work and lovely little readers, such as I never knew. When the weather is rough, we take them with the car. Twice a year the school nurse examines them. When my grandchildren go to school, I hope for perfect lighting and ventilation, for universal hot lunches, for a high school with classic and vocational possibilities—in short, for the equal of any city school.

I know happiness does not rest solely on the question of city or country but I do think that, considering the steady improvement in living conditions on the farm, the greatest possibilities lie in that direction. So I repeat that I hope my daughters may both marry farmers.

Mrs. H. U.
Grand Forks County, N.D.

Storm Signal

[90]

The Heart of a Farmer ...

Basket Weave

[4]

Do I want my daughter to marry a farmer?

I should ask her:

First, is he fit to be the father to your children?

Second, will they be proud to call him Father?

Third, is he kind and considerate?

Fourth, has he strength, courage and ambition enough to make a home, in every sense of the word?

Fifth, is he willing to sacrifice some of his boyhood pleasure for her sake?

Boys on the farm have not the temptations of the city boy and have a cleaner, more wholesome environment.

With few exceptions, the heart of the farmer is in his home; that of his city cousin is too often in a down-town club or playhouse.

Many city mothers are obliged to go out to work, leaving their little ones at the mercy of others or on the streets. On the farm we find more sincerity and closer relationship among

94

friends—our interests being in common. The most lonely life on earth, I think, is that of a stranger in the heart of a big city.

Let us help our husbands by doing our own canning, preserving, sewing; make the cows and chickens feed and clothe us; study up all of the farmer's problems and help our husbands to solve them. Then when election time comes, let us get out and vote for men who understand farming conditions and who will legislate in the interest of the farmer.

Above all, let us not make workshops of our homes. Let us have more community centers, and get out and shake off some of the dust of monotony. Let us have good speakers, good music; read the best books; have programs of spelling matches, debates and current events, and lively community singing. Let us get out of the rut!

 Mrs. A. U.
Ransom County, N.D.

Gentleman's Fancy

[44]

Marry a Good Farmer

Economy

[29]

A home is not a home unless it is full of cheerfulness and kindness. It needs healthy, playing children, the spirit of work and also the spirit of love and inter-responsibility. Where can these essentials be found but in a real home on a farm in the country? The little children get the spirit of work, for each member of the family has his own work to do. How happy a child is when given a calf or pig to raise, the money to be his when the animal is sold. He learns lessons in economy, balanced rations, and so forth. But all is not work. Coasting, skating, tramps into the woods, swimming in the ponds, all tend to build our country boys and girls "fair and true." They get the love of growing things. They learn the cycle of life, the law of reproduction, gradually and in the right way.

The woman is the partner of the farmer, doing as much of the real work as he. She usually does the bookkeeping. All is not easy on the farm but much of the terribly laborious work and long hours have been eliminated by electricity and machinery. The phonograph, the automobile, and the many community houses furnish pleasure for the country people. I have heard city people say they have had more real fun at a church supper in the country than at any entertainment in the city.

The financial problem is always a problem on the farm. It is often, for the young people, a great struggle. They learn many lessons by sad experience. Crops fail, valuable stock dies. Perhaps the husband even has to "work out" during the winter to get money to buy seeds and fertilizers in the spring. But prosperity and all good come to those who work industriously and have within their souls the love of their work. You girls who wish to marry, prepare yourselves and marry a good farmer, if you wish to be healthy, wealthy and wise.

 Mrs. L. H. D.
Worcester County, Mass.

Snowball

[81]

The Role of Helpmeet

Basket

[3]

I s there any other vocation where woman can better fulfill the role of helpmeet than as a farmer's wife?

She must be accomplished, since she must be cook, laundress, nurse, dairymaid, seamstress—besides the care and responsibility that is attendant in every home.

The home of the farmer's wife can have most of the labor-saving devices on the market, good books—plenty of them, the leading magazines, telephone, music, pictures, and so forth—all at a nominal cost. Amusements in the country are more varied than any other place: we have fishing, driving, skating, horseback riding, croquet, tennis, hayrides, corn-roasts, all kinds of picnics, and other good times. There is never a scarcity of refreshments and throughout the summer season, there is fruit. If there are not social advantages in the community, one can start something. The neighbors will be eager to join.

The work of the farmer's wife is often burdensome. This can be helped by the spirit in which it is done and by putting some of the element of play into it. If some task is to be done, attempt it, believing it to be a recreation and notice the difference in your outlook. Since we are only children grown up, and a child is taught to love work by doing it as play, cannot grownups try this a little? Too often we forget that work is a blessing God has given us; that He meant each of us to be a producer—not to be content with doing less than our share. Life is what we make it and the busy person is always a happy one.

In the light of my own experience, it has meant hard work but it has been a most happy life; and I would not want to live anywhere else except on the farm.

MRS. M. M. C.
Allegheny County, Pa.

Shooting Star

[78]

The Joy of Achievement

Spider Legs

[82]

If a young farmer, educated, industrious, honest, congenial, seeks your daughter's hand, straightway procure a minister, give them your blessing and be assured of their happiness.

Life is ennobling to the farmer as he rises in the morning greeted by the sun's beauty and the voices of his "dumb" friends. After his chores and a comfortable breakfast he goes forth with trusty horses or efficient tractor. In every move he comes in contact with Nature, so full of lessons for the receptive mind. Useless to him is the tiny city lot and in comparison the city itself is cramped and narrow.

Our cities and the interesting life they offer are vital to our Nation; equally so are the rural districts the bulwark of our existence. Each has a bright and dark side. But as I review my own years, I recall the joy of achievement, the absorbing interest of community building, the neighborliness of my sister farm women, the blessedness of homemaking in the one real place for a home. I forgot there were times when the toil seemed hard and the years seemed long and I rejoice in the New Day for the farmer and his wife. The future is brighter, the opportunity for service greater year by year. Our organizations, the Grange[8], Farm Bureau[2], numerous farm clubs, good roads, good schools, churches, and countless other elements of progress are enriching farm life and assuring us that so far as these things may influence life, satisfaction for herself and service to others await the girl who would make the farm her home. Yes, I *do* want her to be a farmer's wife.

 MRS. W. B. McC.
Fulton County, Ohio

Wedding Ring

[101]

101

A Vote for the Country

Flower Garden Path

[36]

Rural families can enjoy unlimited companionship. City men are away from their families all day and for at least one, and often two meals, where farm people eat three happy, chatty meals together nearly every day. There are many little surprise trips, when the jitney[9] is taken, just so "Mamma and the children can have a ride."

Perhaps the privacy and seclusion will appeal to my daughter as strongly as it does to me. It is blessed peace of mind to know that a door may slam, a child cry, or a belated washing be hung on the line without attracting the attention of neighbors. The children play out of doors with no temptation to run off and no doubtful playmates for me to worry about. Their playground is acres of grass and trees instead of a plot of bluegrass, a strip of sidewalk and the street. When the little ones are coming, timidity about seeing people does not keep the farm mother from walks in the fresh air and, at the last, the stork's arrival is not a neighborhood affair. Oh, the peace and quiet of my rural home at such trying times! Where children are concerned, it is a vote for the country, every time.

 MRS. A. B.
Marion County, Kan.

Wild Rose & Square

[106]

A Cultured Woman

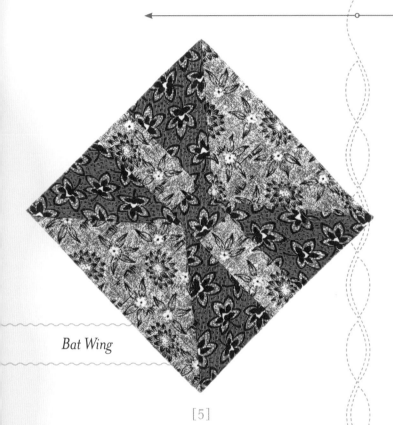

Bat Wing

[5]

I hope to see my daughters, three in number, marry farmers, and I'm not so particular about any special sort of farming. All I ask is that it be a farm in a good productive place, and I am sure that my daughter will be where she will have the freedom so many women of today are going to town to find.

People are mistaken who say farm women are slaves. Farm women have hard work at times, or our work is such that we have to hurry up a little but we have time to read, do fancy work, play with our children and make their clothes in the latest fashion. We have everything in our homes that our city sisters have, and all that nature can give us. Besides when our day's work is done we ride or sit in the open, quiet fresh air, with mind and muscle relaxed and so can solve hard problems with no effort.

I want my daughter to be a cultured woman; a cultured person must be a thinker and I am sure there is no other place or work which affords the chance for one to think than the farm does.

Men and women have a right to salvage from their business time hours in which to created the right sort of home atmosphere, to enrich surroundings so that children may get their ideals in the home, their taste for beauty, books and standards of life, not deriving these things from shop windows, movies, billboards and jazz music, but from refined, cultured, country, farm homes.

Women of today have greater opportunities and greater knowledge but our problems are more difficult. We must be thinkers in order to build for the health, happiness and success of tomorrow. The farm woman has the time and the place for this thought.

 Mrs. J. A. M.
Ingham County, Mich.

Spool

[84]

Sharing His Work, Pleasure and Problems

Friendship Star

[41]

If my daughter has truly found the right man in her farmer, she will have the best opportunity for ideal companionship. She can be his helpmate in every sense of the word, sharing his work, pleasures and problems, and justly earning a share of credit for his accomplishment. There will be long weeks of hard work and hours of discouragement but there will also be many days when relaxation will come with a knowledge of work well done, with pleasant visiting back and forth among neighbors, with books and magazines, community club meetings, and lectures and entertainments, that will all make one's efforts seem worthwhile.

She will have the best place in the world to raise her children. They will have all out-doors to play and grow in. They will learn nature's lessons naturally and normally, without acquiring wrong and oftentimes soul-blighting conceptions of life's wonders.

My daughter and her husband will find in their rural life, recognition for their real abilities. And what true friends they will find! Lack of wealth will not restrict them, nor lack of "style" prevent their social success. If they are thinkers and workers, and anxious for the betterment of the community, how eagerly their assistance and advice will be called for! They will find ample opportunity for developing faculties of leadership and organization. More and more, the farmers of this country are acquiring prominence in adjusting the affairs of the nation and of the world. National leaders are discovering that the farmer, with his problems and attainments, is one of the most vital cogs in the wheels of state.

MRS. J. M. V.
Pocahontas County, Iowa

Wild Geese

[104]

Rich in Blessings

Homeward Bound

Please give me the country every time. And I have chosen it for my dear little, adopted daughter who, after five years on the farm, loves it as I do.

I was born and raised on a farm but grew up knowing absolutely nothing about it. My parents, educated, cultured Virginians of the old school, were not disposed to let me go over the place. If I even so much as put foot in the barn lot, my father said: "Now, little daughter, run to the house with your mother." There were few good roads, no cars, not many telephones, so the farm was jail to me—I hated it. By the time I was grown I would willingly have given my interest in the home place to anybody that would accept. The beautiful meadows, the orchard, the cool, deep woods—none of it for me. But then came a change. My mother died. Father was an invalid and my own health bad. He and I spent a winter in the city and there the scales fell from my eyes. I saw his longing for the old home, and I *felt* my longing, so back we came. His joy was indescribable, and mine was almost equal. Life was a revelation to me. How near I had come to losing the very best opportunities ever offered to me!

I now have happiness, health, content—three blessings I had scarcely known before. There have been innumerable obstacles but each one overcome has made me stronger. I have gardened, milked, canned, built fences, sheds, split wood—anything to get along because I loved the farm and was determined to succeed if my efforts would mean success.

CONTINUED

Sawtooth

[76]

Buckwheat

[13]

Country life calls for all the ingenuity and resource there is in you. Things are subject to sudden change and you have got to meet the emergency with whatever is at hand. No stores right around the corner to supply every needed, and many unnecessary, wants! Use your brains instead!

It is a wonderful thing to see the fruits of your labor, crops, livestock, grow day by day and to experience at the same time, love, reverence and wonder, at the Giver of all.

Farms can have all the conveniences and comforts of town homes, with the added luxuries of the restfulness of the country. Good roads are becoming prevalent and automobiles have eliminated distance. My girl's happiness is great to behold, when she comes in from a ride on a load of hay or the tractor-plow, wheat drill or corn planter. She knows and goes all the rounds a great deal more at ten years of age than I did at twenty-five. I am raising her to be a good wife for a good farmer, for there is where I believe she will find greatest happiness and usefulness. She will go to him prepared for life as far as I am able to teach her and have her taught. Oh, if I could only make people realize how full of possibility is the country life and how rich in blessings.

M. R. G.
Roanoke County, Va.

Waste Not

[97]

An Ever-Changing Delight

Swallow

[93]

The public traveling libraries bring the best of literature to the farms, and the farm mother has a chance such as no other has, to guide her children's taste in reading to that which is best. The women on the farm do not need to turn to the movies or bridge to find change. No two days' work are ever alike. And the view from her window is an ever-changing delight of cloud and sky, tree and field. To have a part in all the activities of the farm is Life and, if a woman wills, Life at its best.

I think the woman who is a failure on the farm would be a failure in town. But there is no doubt that some find a satisfying happiness on a farm that others could not.

It is impossible for me to see what ten years or more may bring but by the past ten years' advance in agricultural life, I feel that the advantages of the farmer's wife will be proportionately greater. The dividing line between city and country is growing less clearly defined.

The chances are that my daughters will look upon electric lights, water systems, furnaces, power washers and automobiles as we regarded a hand-run washer, gasoline lamp, pump in the kitchen, oil stove and a covered carriage. We once considered them luxuries on the farm but now they are necessities, only we substitute an auto for the carriage.

I hope first that my future son-in-law will be an upright, honest man and worthy of my daughter, and she worthy of him; and next, I hope he will be a farmer.

 MRS. E. F.
Portage County, Wis.

Wood Lily

[110]

Emphatically, Yes!

Old Windmill

[62]

Do I want my daughter to marry a farmer? Emphatically, yes! I want her to lead the life her father and mother have led, plus the added capacity for living which her superior education has given her.

The farmer's wife today has plenty of work but, rightly managed, there is no drudgery. Electric light plants light our homes, wash, iron, sweep and pump water for house use. Other labor-savers reduce our work, not to the standard of a crocheting, gossiping, and shopping routine, thank God! but to the place where with work systematized and each child assigned tasks proportionate to his size, we have time for recreation and the enjoyment of our families.

Recreation on the farm—or rather lack of it—does not trouble us as it does some. With good roads and automobiles we are able to be associated with the activities of the Grange[7], Farm Bureau[2], church, school, Boy Scouts and farm women's club. However, we are still old fashioned enough to believe in spending the majority of our evenings at home. Games, good music and good reading in the home have always attracted our family rather than the cheap movie and the village dance hall. Our centralized school compares very favorable with any city school.

CONTINUED

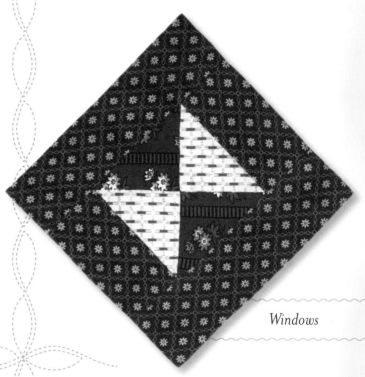

Windows

[109]

115

Streak of Lightning

[92]

The farmer of today, to be successful, must be educated, alert and scientific in his methods. He rotates his crops, keeps the purebred stock and does a large part of his work with a tractor. We all realize the farmer is facing the darkest hour in the history of our nation, but behind this cloud we see him coming into his own in Congress, and with the backing of the Farm Bureau[2], he will keep it. This forecasts the brightest future agriculture has ever seen. The right kind of prices and markets must and will come. But even times of depression can not materially affect the farmer's living as they do the city man's, for he has his food from his own soil, vegetables, fruits, grains, milk and meats; so, financially, I would say his is the most independent of occupations.

I want my daughter to marry a farmer that they may live and work together in God's free air and sunshine. Here is happiness. Here is health. The wonders of nature are all about them, and even God Himself seems nearer here. In no other occupation can there be such co-operation and understanding between the work of husband and wife. Their children, from their earliest years, grow up as partners of their work and their joys. No other conditions could be more suited toward fostering the mental and moral development of our future generation.

 Mrs. S. M. M.
Franklin County, Ohio

Whirlpool

[102]

Enjoy Life to the Fullest

Calico Puzzle

[16]

The farmer I married twelve years ago has a large farm which is "The Old Home Place" in his family. The fourth generation is now growing up here. It is a choice location, six miles from town. There is a beautiful lawn and drive, with fine old shade trees; a small park with a miniature lake; and a fine, large orchard. The house is colonial in style and has every modern convenience. Each year improvements are added in farm buildings. We are all proud of our horses, fine herds of registered Herefords, Poland China hogs and Hampshire sheep. Our children never want for ideal playgrounds or wholesome recreation. Our three daughters are growing up with a love and reverence for their home that is not often found in city homes. Temptations for wrong doing are not on every side. They are not spoiled by jazz music and dances. They do not have the "movie habit" with its question-able influence, nor are they in the company of undesirable associates. In our home we have the best music, a piano, a phonograph, a bookcase filled with good books, our library table covered with many of the best magazines and papers.

The farmer's wife of the past endured great hardships. Two generations ago the farmer's education was meager. It was almost impossible to attend church or any public meeting. The farmer's wife had never dreamed of home conveniences. The home and home grounds were unattractive. In those days the country woman almost always wore an ugly calico "wrapper" and her one "Sunday dress" was worn for years. Besides doing her duty as a neighbor, her outside work and influence were very limited.

The farmer's wife of today enjoys life to the fullest. Her opportunities are limited only by time and strength. Yes, I hope my daughter marries the man of my dreams—the farmer of tomorrow—and "lives happily ever after" in the home of my dream—the country home of the future.

 Mrs. C. K. T.
Newton County, Ind.

Ozark Maple Leaf

[63]

A Good and Useful Life

*Butterfly
at the Crossroads*

[14]

The farmer's wife, as a class, is now nearly unacquainted with the wash tub, of hauling water in a pail and a thousand other dreary tasks. A turn of the faucet gives water; the pressure of a button gives light, runs the washing machine, flat iron, churn, separator and so forth; furnaces, bathrooms and septic tanks are recognized necessities being fast installed on every farm. Milady of the farm has oilstoves, pressure cookers or fireless cookers. She has time to attend fairs, enjoy the newspaper, hear good music and manicure her finger nails. Her family has an acquaintance with nature that can not be obtained elsewhere. The abundance of fresh air, eggs, cream, garden stuff, needs no comment.

You may say every farm woman does not have all these conveniences. Neither has every city woman. In listing a few of the comforts of the farmer's wife, I have not listed any of the discomforts I may fancy my city friend labors under. If she is happy and I am happy, why disturb this happiness? On a short trip in any direction we see farm homes that fairly radiate comfort and happiness and beauty, and as I wish my daughter to lead a good and useful life, one of which it may truly be said when she departs, "the world is better for her having lived in it," I hope she will marry a farmer.

Mrs. M. A. D.
Sargent County, N.D.

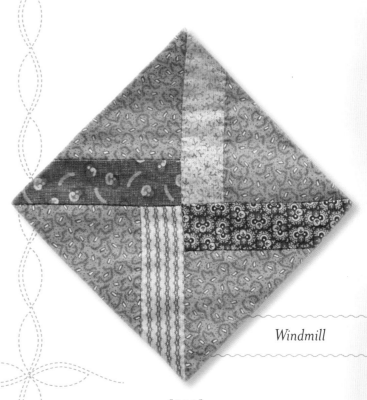

Windmill

[108]

Searching for the Happiest Life in the World

Noon & Light

[60]

As I write I think of different things, of the eggs turned so carefully that haven't hatched well, of the turkeys that have disappeared, causing futile searches through the tall, wet grass and blighting hopes for the new kitchen linoleum or a washing machine.

I think of the steers that develop blackleg, the hogs that grunt healthily one morning and die the next. I see my husband come home at dusk, walking behind the tired horses, face dusty and drawn under the two-year-old straw hat, knowing that the price he'll get for his corn doesn't warrant his labor. The cows that don't "pay out" stand there waiting, an extra hour's chores night and morning. I think of the hired men that quit in the busiest season or who mutter darkly about chores. There are the times when the very knowledge that we can and do raise good hogs and cattle makes us discouraged—we can't make 'em worth what they should be. There are those unbearable periods when tired out, we see the town folks jaunt off at five for a picnic or to enjoy a game of tennis. Do we feel our inefficiency when city friends say, "Why does John insist on farming?"

Then I remember the spring mornings, gorgeous dawns, cows standing mild-eyed and ruminant as they let down the streams that mean puddings and cream, the hired man whistling, the husband cheered by the day and—the muffins. I think of the dishes and the separator washed, vegetables bubbling on the range, the cream pie that the family is *crazy* about all ready for dinner, the cool porch and the peeps at the magazines. I hear eldest daughter practising while a thrush from the lilac bush ventures variations.

CONTINUED

Whirlwind

[103]

Autumn Tints

[2]

From the orchard I hear the shrill, happy voices of the birds and the younger children. I see the wise old hen leading her family toward me as I come in from the garden—no scratching for her when living comes easy! The fall days, busy, too busy to worry over prices. Threshing, silo filling, pies, cakes, brown baked beans, steaming platters of meat, hungry men, fresh bread, more coffee. Hard work—that is the essence of life. Winter—Farm Bureau[2], doughnuts, laughter, earnest discussion, Susie struggling over long division, frosty drives to gay dinners, corn popping on the kitchen range, everyone talking at once. Then quiet and we settle down, Friend Husband with his farm paper, Friend Wife with a pair of mutilated overalls.

"I see," says Friend Husband, "that this fellow predicts a better year. He says," etc., etc.

And Friend Wife, although she'd prefer Einstein or the cure for leprosy just for a change, sets her patch and replies eagerly, "I think he's right!"

"Next spring," begins the husband, and he is launched, ever optimistic, eager for the work he so earnestly believes in.

Would I have my daughter marry a farmer? Yes—if she is strong, and eager to work; if she is searching for the happiest life in the world; if she wants a husband with the ability and desire to use his body as well as his brains; if she can take his disappointments as well as joys. And all our daughters are eager and strong. All of them are looking for full, useful lives—we farmers bring 'em up that way.

Mrs. H. St. C.
Franklin County, Iowa

Friendship Block

[40]

A Garden Paradise

Star of Hope

[88]

I want my daughter to marry a farmer because she is a farm girl. Her home life and school work have trained her for farm life.

I hope her husband will be a farmer because farmers are producers and givers of life. I believe that farming is the backbone of the world's progress and prosperity. It is not only life-giving but furnishes the power for all higher vocations of the mind. Each person's destiny must come indirectly from the soil. So I see the patient tillers of the soil back of the poets, the musicians and artists. And I also see the world's great economic problems and many of its social ones, worked out through the products the soil and their producers.

So, not for the money nor the fame, but because of the vital need for the work; because I believe the job of farming gives a sturdy individuality and breeds hope and courage in its workers; because of the peace and tranquility that comes as a reward and a benediction to those who follow God's plan to make a paradise in a garden, I am hoping my daughter may marry a farmer.

 Mrs. J.B.
Polk County, Wis.

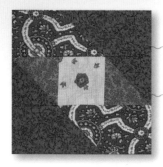

[1] *Attic Windows*

BLOCK ASSEMBLY

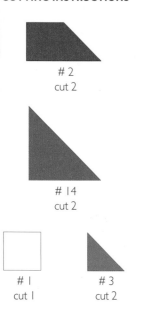

2
cut 2

14
cut 2

1
cut 1

3
cut 2

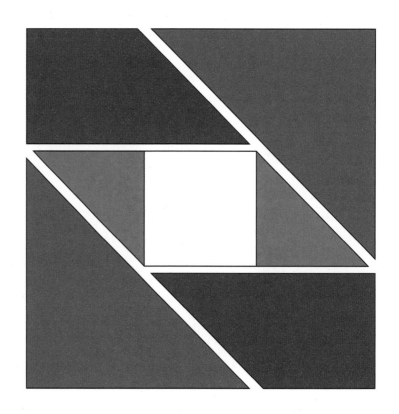

[2] *Autumn Tints*

BLOCK ASSEMBLY

5
cut 2

4
cut 4

4
cut 2

4
cut 2

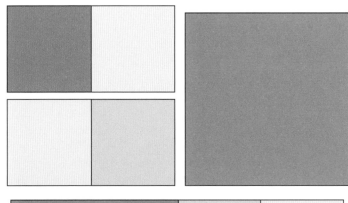

[3] *Basket*

BLOCK ASSEMBLY

TEMPLATE NUMBERS & CUTTING INSTRUCTIONS

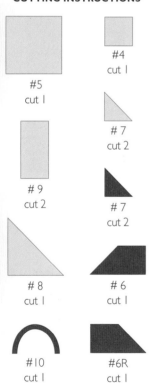

#5
cut 1

#4
cut 1

7
cut 2

9
cut 2

7
cut 2

8
cut 1

6
cut 1

#10
cut 1

#6R
cut 1

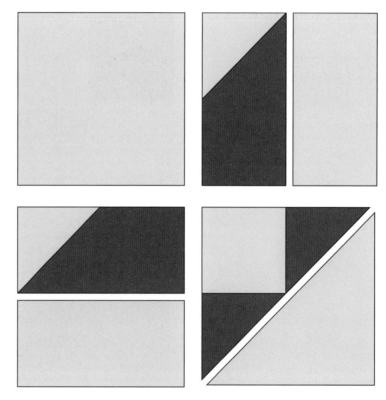

Note: The light-blue/dark-blue rectangular units are mirror images.

[4] *Basket Weave*

BLOCK ASSEMBLY

TEMPLATE NUMBERS & CUTTING INSTRUCTIONS

#11
cut 4

#11
cut 4

#11
cut 4

[5] *Bat Wing*

BLOCK ASSEMBLY

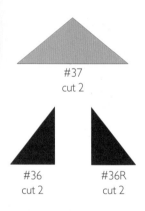

#37
cut 2

#36
cut 2

#36R
cut 2

#35
cut 2

#34
cut 1

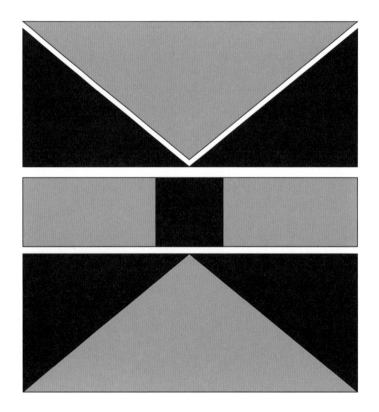

[6] *Big Dipper*

BLOCK ASSEMBLY

**TEMPLATE NUMBERS &
CUTTING INSTRUCTIONS**

#12
cut 8

#12
cut 8

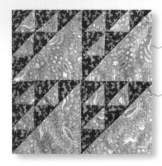

[7] *Birds in the Air*

BLOCK ASSEMBLY

#8
cut 4

#13
cut 12

#13
cut 24

[8] *Bouquet*

BLOCK ASSEMBLY

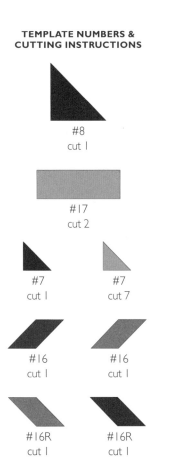

**TEMPLATE NUMBERS &
CUTTING INSTRUCTIONS**

#8
cut 1

#17
cut 2

#7
cut 1

#7
cut 7

#16
cut 1

#16
cut 1

#16R
cut 1

#16R
cut 1

Note: The tan/gold units are mirror images

[9] *Box*

BLOCK ASSEMBLY

#3
cut 8

#3
cut 8

#1
cut 1

[10] *Bowtie*

**TEMPLATE NUMBERS &
CUTTING INSTRUCTIONS**

#7
cut 4

#18
cut 2

#18
cut 2

[11] *Broken Dishes*

BLOCK ASSEMBLY

#7
cut 16

#7
cut 16

[12] *Broken Sugar Bowl*

BLOCK ASSEMBLY

TEMPLATE NUMBERS & CUTTING INSTRUCTIONS

#1
cut 2

#19
cut 4

#3
cut 4

#19
cut 4

#3
cut 4

#19
cut 4

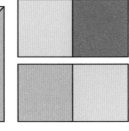

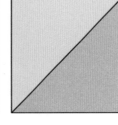

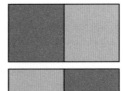

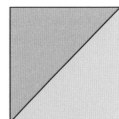

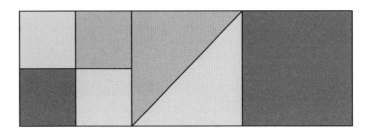

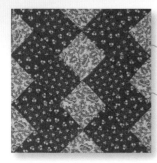

[13] *Buckwheat*

BLOCK ASSEMBLY

#20
cut 12

#20
cut 8

#20
cut 8

#21
cut 2

#21
cut 2

140

[14] *Butterfly at the Crossroads*

BLOCK ASSEMBLY

TEMPLATE NUMBERS & CUTTING INSTRUCTIONS

#38
cut 8

#38
cut 8

#35
cut 4

#34
cut 4

#34
cut 5

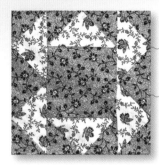

[15] *Buzzard's Roost*

BLOCK ASSEMBLY

#5
cut 1

#12
cut 2

#12
cut 6

7
cut 8

[16] *Calico Puzzle*

BLOCK ASSEMBLY

TEMPLATE NUMBERS & CUTTING INSTRUCTIONS

#3
cut 4

#3
cut 4

#1
cut 4

#1
cut 1

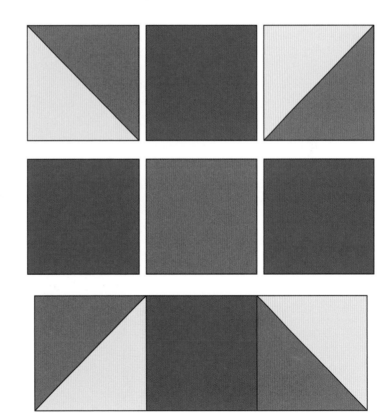

[17] *Cats & Mice*

BLOCK ASSEMBLY

#15
cut 4

#21
cut 5

#13
cut 12

#13
cut 8

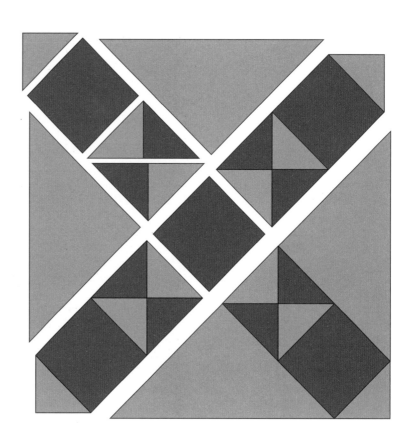

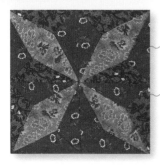

[18] *Century of Progress*

BLOCK ASSEMBLY

#23
cut 3

#23
cut 5

#23R
cut 3

#23R
cut 5

#24
cut 8

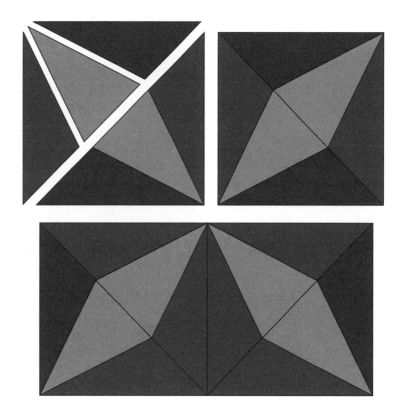

[19] *Checkerboard*

BLOCK ASSEMBLY

TEMPLATE NUMBERS & CUTTING INSTRUCTIONS

#20
cut 8

#13
cut 4

#21
cut 4

#21
cut 1

#21
cut 2

#21
cut 2

#21
cut 2

#21
cut 2

[20] *Churn Dash*

BLOCK ASSEMBLY

TEMPLATE NUMBERS & CUTTING INSTRUCTIONS

#3
cut 4

#3
cut 4

#1
cut 1

#25
cut 4

#25
cut 4

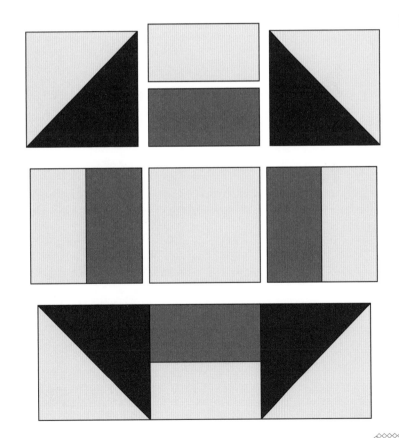

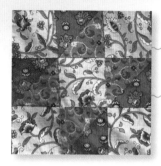

[21] *Contrary Wife*

BLOCK ASSEMBLY

#3
cut 4

#3
cut 4

#1
cut 5

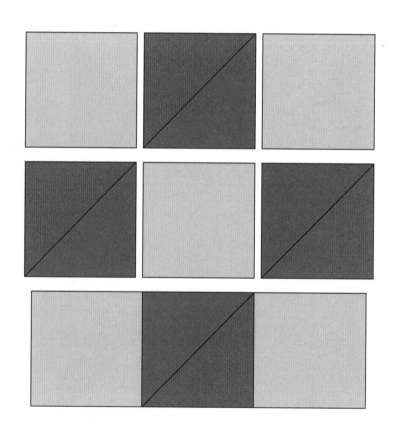

[22] Corn & Beans

BLOCK ASSEMBLY

TEMPLATE NUMBERS & CUTTING INSTRUCTIONS

#3
cut 2

#3
cut 6

#20
cut 4

#13
cut 20

#13
cut 12

[23] *Country Farm*

BLOCK ASSEMBLY

#1
cut 4

#20
cut 4

#20
cut 8

#3
cut 2

#3
cut 2

[24] *Country Path*

BLOCK ASSEMBLY

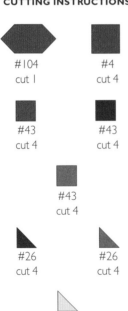

#104
cut 1

#4
cut 4

#43
cut 4

#43
cut 4

#43
cut 4

#26
cut 4

#26
cut 4

#26
cut 10

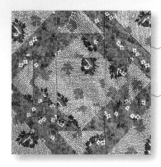

[25] *Cups & Saucers*

BLOCK ASSEMBLY

**TEMPLATE NUMBERS &
CUTTING INSTRUCTIONS**

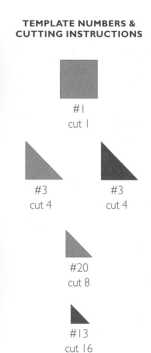

#1
cut 1

#3
cut 4

#3
cut 4

#20
cut 8

#13
cut 16

[26] *Cut Glass Dish*

BLOCK ASSEMBLY

TEMPLATE NUMBERS & CUTTING INSTRUCTIONS

#1
cut 3

#13
cut 24

#13
cut 24

[27] *Darting Birds*

BLOCK ASSEMBLY

#19
cut 4

#19
cut 4

#3
cut 4

#13
cut 24

#13
cut 16

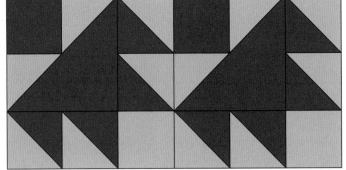

154

[28] *Duck and Ducklings*

BLOCK ASSEMBLY

**TEMPLATE NUMBERS &
CUTTING INSTRUCTIONS**

#38
cut 4

#38
cut 12

#33
cut 4

#34
cut 4

#34
cut 5

155

[29] *Economy*

BLOCK ASSEMBLY

**TEMPLATE NUMBERS &
CUTTING INSTRUCTIONS**

#8
cut 4

#5
cut 1

#12
cut 4

[30] *End of Day*

BLOCK ASSEMBLY

TEMPLATE NUMBERS & CUTTING INSTRUCTIONS

#6
cut 4

#6R
cut 4

#7
cut 4

#7
cut 4

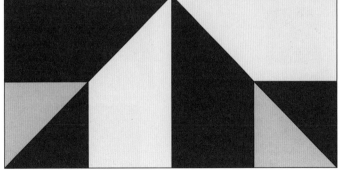

[31] *Evening Star*

BLOCK ASSEMBLY

TEMPLATE NUMBERS & CUTTING INSTRUCTIONS

#12
cut 4

#7
cut 8

#5
cut 1

#4
cut 4

[32] *Farmer's Daughter*

BLOCK ASSEMBLY

TEMPLATE NUMBERS & CUTTING INSTRUCTIONS

#38
cut 8

#38
cut 8

#34
cut 4

#34
cut 8

#34
cut 5

[33] *Farmer's Puzzle*

BLOCK ASSEMBLY

#32
cut 4

#32R
cut 4

#31
cut 16

#29
cut 1

#30
cut 2

[34] *Flock*

BLOCK ASSEMBLY

**TEMPLATE NUMBERS &
CUTTING INSTRUCTIONS**

#8
cut 2

#8
cut 2

#7
cut 8

#7
cut 8

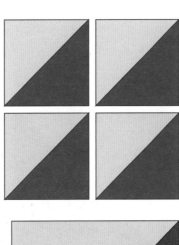

[35] *Flower Basket*

BLOCK ASSEMBLY

TEMPLATE NUMBERS & CUTTING INSTRUCTIONS

#1
cut 3

#39
cut 1

#39
cut 1

#3
cut 2

#3
cut 2

#105
cut 1

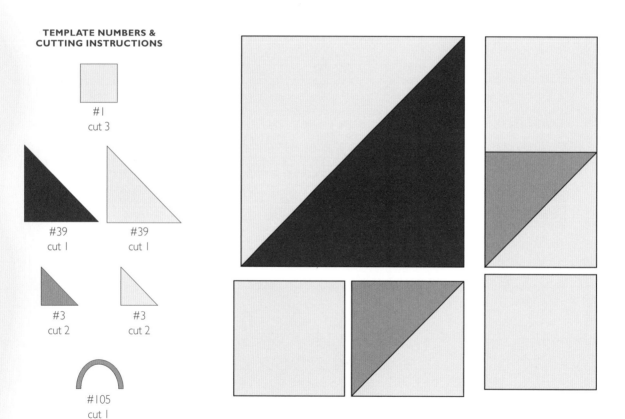

[36] *Flower Garden Path*

BLOCK ASSEMBLY

TEMPLATE NUMBERS & CUTTING INSTRUCTIONS

#20
cut 4

#13
cut 20

#13
cut 8

#19
cut 4

#44
cut 4

#25
cut 2

[37] *Flower Pot*

BLOCK ASSEMBLY

TEMPLATE NUMBERS & CUTTING INSTRUCTIONS

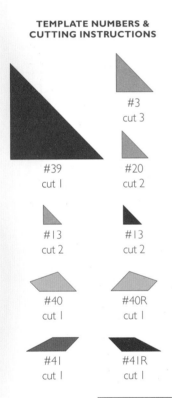

#39
cut 1

#3
cut 3

#20
cut 2

#13
cut 2

#13
cut 2

#40
cut 1

#40R
cut 1

#41
cut 1

#41R
cut 1

#42
cut 2

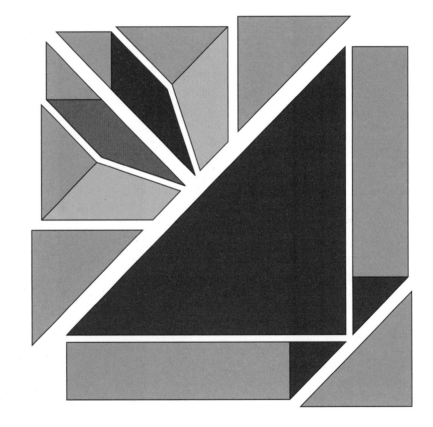

[38] *Four Winds*

BLOCK ASSEMBLY

#19
cut 4

#19
cut 4

#13
cut 8

#13
cut 26

#13
cut 8

#13
cut 14

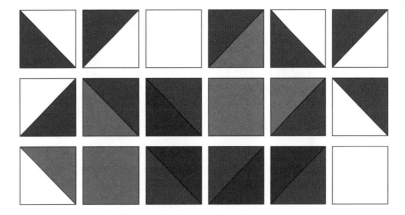

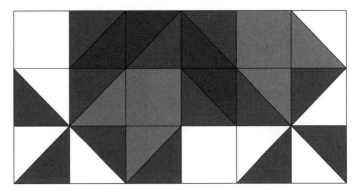

Note: The bottom half is the same as the top half rotated 180°

[39] *Friendship*

BLOCK ASSEMBLY

TEMPLATE NUMBERS & CUTTING INSTRUCTIONS

#8
cut 1

#8
cut 1

#8
cut 1

#8
cut 1

#7
cut 1

#7
cut 1

#7
cut 1

#7
cut 1

#45
cut 4

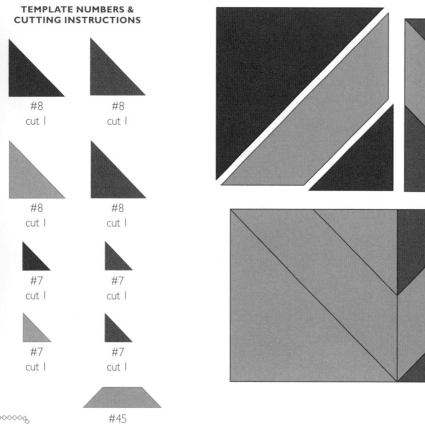

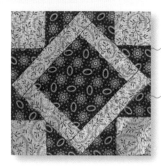

[40] *Friendship Block*

**TEMPLATE NUMBERS &
CUTTING INSTRUCTIONS**

#7
cut 8

#103
cut 1

#4
cut 4

#27
cut 2

#28
cut 2

[41] *Friendship Star*

BLOCK ASSEMBLY

#1
cut 1

#1
cut 4

#3
cut 4

#3
cut 4

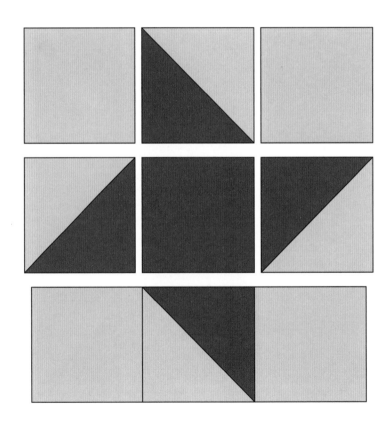

[42] *Fruit Basket*

BLOCK ASSEMBLY

TEMPLATE NUMBERS & CUTTING INSTRUCTIONS

#46
cut 1

#46R
cut 1

#38
cut 7

#33
cut 1

#33
cut 1

#47
cut 2

#34
cut 2

#38
cut 10

#38
cut 3

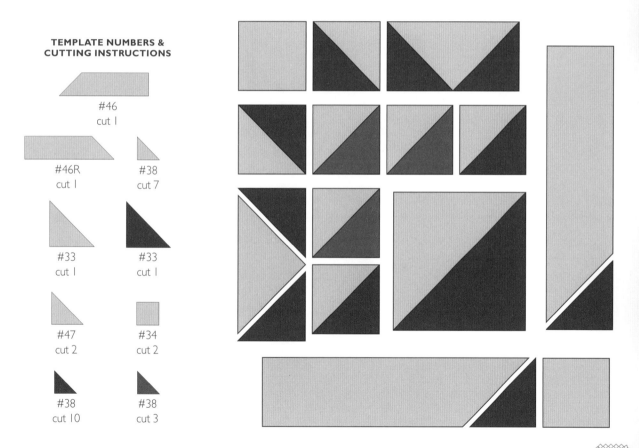

[43] *Garden Path*

BLOCK ASSEMBLY

TEMPLATE NUMBERS & CUTTING INSTRUCTIONS

#19
cut 2

#19
cut 2

#19
cut 2

#19
cut 2

#13
cut 20

#13
cut 2

#13
cut 2

#13
cut 2

#13
cut 2

#44
cut 4

#7
cut 4

[44] *Gentleman's Fancy*

BLOCK ASSEMBLY

#1
cut 1

#3
cut 8

#49
cut 4

#20
cut 4

[45] *Grape Basket*

BLOCK ASSEMBLY

TEMPLATE NUMBERS & CUTTING INSTRUCTIONS

#34
cut 1

#48
cut 2

#33
cut 2

#33
cut 1

#38
cut 11

#38
cut 2

#38
cut 11

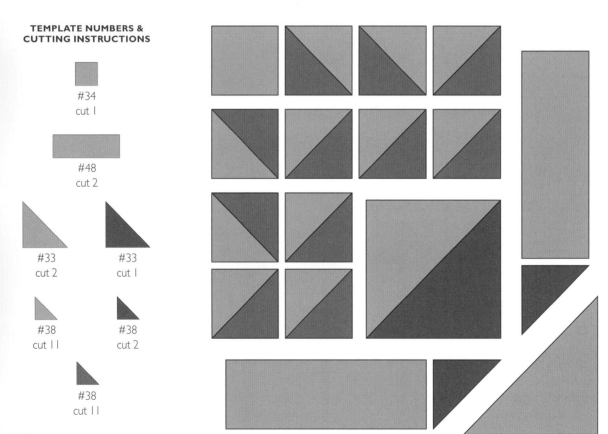

[46] *Hill & Valley*

BLOCK ASSEMBLY

**TEMPLATE NUMBERS &
CUTTING INSTRUCTIONS**

#21
cut 2

#8
cut 4

#3
cut 4

#20
cut 4

#20
cut 2

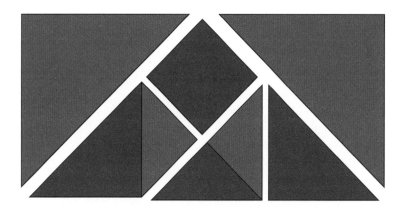

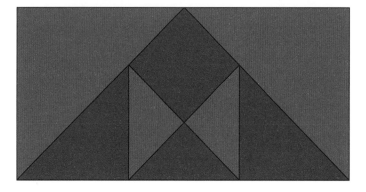

[47] *Homemaker*

BLOCK ASSEMBLY

#53
cut 4

#1
cut 1

#55
cut 4

#55R
cut 4

#54
cut 4

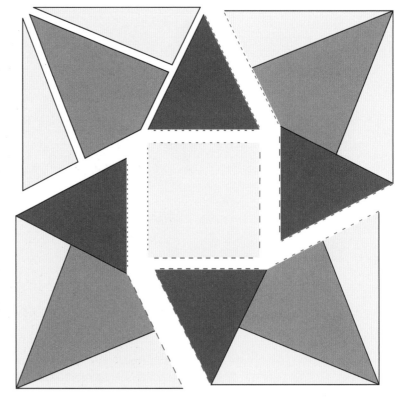

Note: 1. Assemble the four corner units, as shown in the upper-left corner of the block. 2. Join the purple triangles to the center square, as shown by the blue lines. 3. Join the sides of the corner units, as shown by the red lines.

[48] *Homeward Bound*

BLOCK ASSEMBLY

#1
cut 4

#1
cut 1

#19
cut 4

#19
cut 12

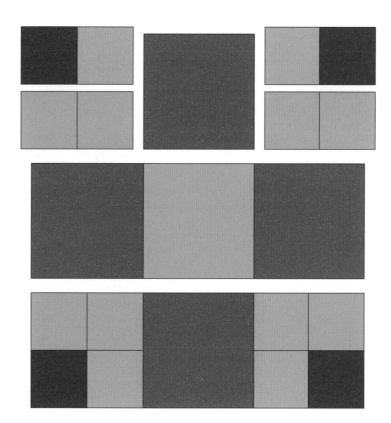

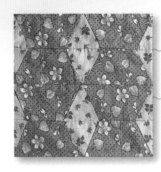

[49] *Honeycomb*

BLOCK ASSEMBLY

TEMPLATE NUMBERS & CUTTING INSTRUCTIONS

#56
cut 8

#57
cut 8

#57R
cut 8

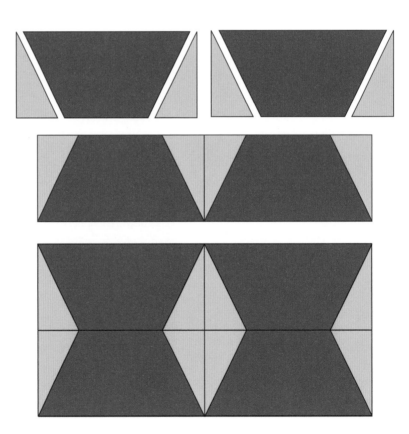

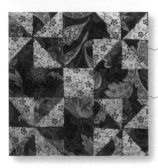

[50] *Honey's Choice*

BLOCK ASSEMBLY

**TEMPLATE NUMBERS &
CUTTING INSTRUCTIONS**

#38
cut 16

#38
cut 16

#35
cut 4

#34
cut 1

[51] *Hovering Birds*

BLOCK ASSEMBLY

#8
cut 2

#4
cut 4

#7
cut 6

#7
cut 10

Note: The bottom half is the same as the top half rotated 180°

[52] *Hovering Hawks*

BLOCK ASSEMBLY

#4
cut 4

#58
cut 2

#7
cut 10

#7
cut 8

Note: The bottom half is the same as the top half rotated 180°

[53] *Jackknife*

BLOCK ASSEMBLY

TEMPLATE NUMBERS & CUTTING INSTRUCTIONS

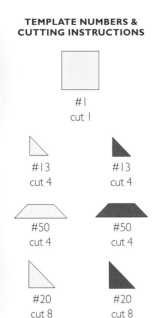

#1
cut 1

#13
cut 4

#13
cut 4

#50
cut 4

#50
cut 4

#20
cut 8

#20
cut 8

BLOCK ASSEMBLY

TEMPLATE NUMBERS & CUTTING INSTRUCTIONS

#1
cut 1

#3
cut 4

#49
cut 4

#51
cut 2

#25
cut 2

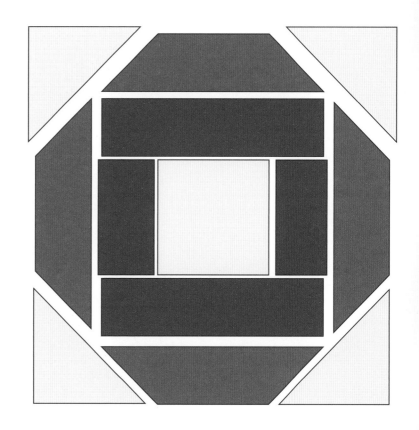

181

[55] *Linoleum*

BLOCK ASSEMBLY

TEMPLATE NUMBERS & CUTTING INSTRUCTIONS

#1
cut 1

#13
cut 8

#25
cut 4

#25
cut 4

#65
cut 4

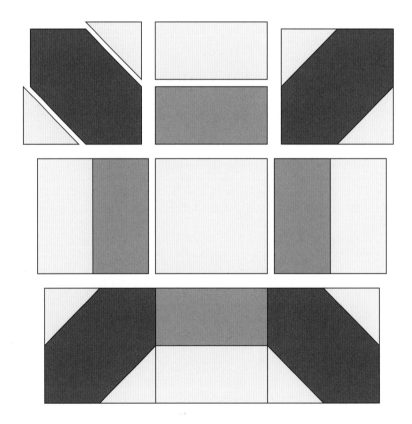

[56] *Maple Leaf*

BLOCK ASSEMBLY

TEMPLATE NUMBERS & CUTTING INSTRUCTIONS

#3
cut 4

#3
cut 4

#7
cut 2

#1
cut 1

#1
cut 3

#52
cut 1

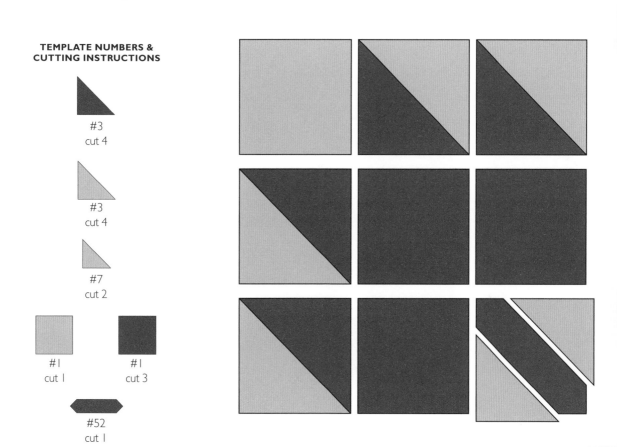

[57] *Morning*

BLOCK ASSEMBLY

TEMPLATE NUMBERS & CUTTING INSTRUCTIONS

#13
cut 16

#20
cut 4

#20
cut 8

#1
cut 1

#19
cut 4

#25
cut 4

[58] *Mother's Dream*

BLOCK ASSEMBLY

TEMPLATE NUMBERS & CUTTING INSTRUCTIONS

#60
cut 1

#12
cut 4

#7
cut 4

#59
cut 4

#59
cut 4

[59] *Night & Day*

BLOCK ASSEMBLY

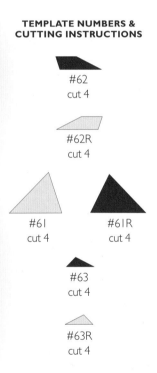

#62
cut 4

#62R
cut 4

#61
cut 4

#61R
cut 4

#63
cut 4

#63R
cut 4

[60] *Noon & Light*

BLOCK ASSEMBLY

**TEMPLATE NUMBERS &
CUTTING INSTRUCTIONS**

#4
cut 4

#45
cut 4

#7
cut 4

#26
cut 8

#26
cut 8

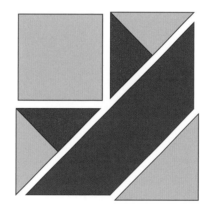

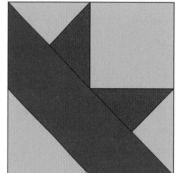

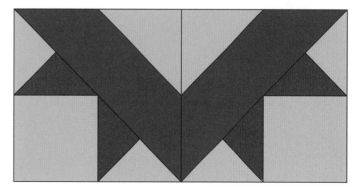

[61] *Northern Lights*

BLOCK ASSEMBLY

#8
cut 2

#8
cut 2

#4
cut 4

#4
cut 4

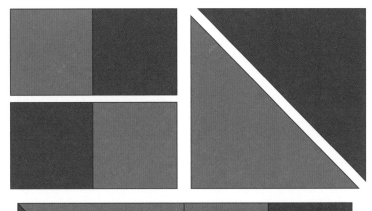

[62] *Old Windmill*

BLOCK ASSEMBLY

#7
cut 16

#7
cut 4

#7
cut 4

#7
cut 4

#7
cut 4

Note: The bottom row is the same as the top row rotated 180°

[63] *Ozark Maple Leaf*

BLOCK ASSEMBLY

TEMPLATE NUMBERS & CUTTING INSTRUCTIONS

#13
cut 4

#13
cut 4

#25
cut 2

#25
cut 2

#11
cut 2

#11
cut 2

#65
cut 2

#65
cut 2

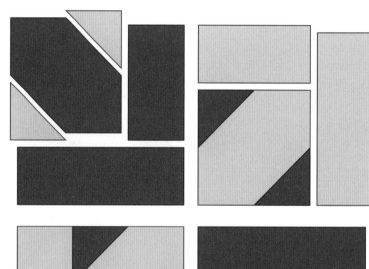

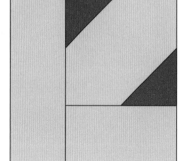

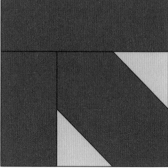

[64] *Peace & Plenty*

BLOCK ASSEMBLY

#7
cut 16

#7
cut 16

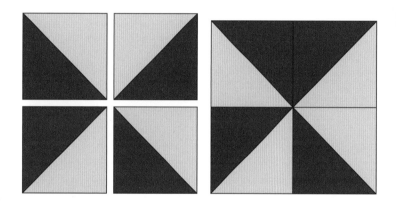

[65] *Peaceful Hours*

BLOCK ASSEMBLY

#69
cut 1

#67
cut 4

#67R
cut 4

#7
cut 4

#7
cut 4

#66
cut 4

#66R
cut 4

#68
cut 12

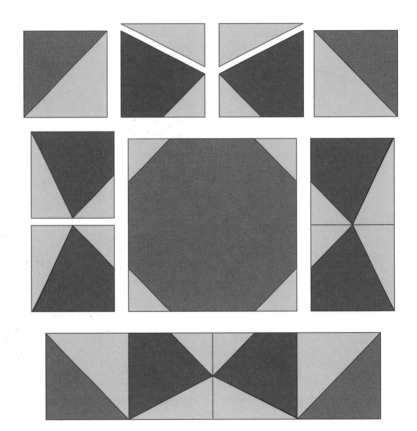

192

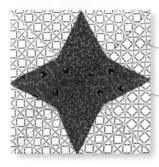

[66] *Periwinkle*

BLOCK ASSEMBLY

**TEMPLATE NUMBERS &
CUTTING INSTRUCTIONS**

#61
cut 4

#61R
cut 4

#70
cut 2

#70
cut 2

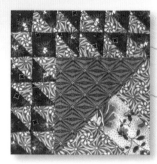

[67] *Pine Tree*

BLOCK ASSEMBLY

TEMPLATE NUMBERS & CUTTING INSTRUCTIONS

#14
cut 1

#12
cut 2

#64
cut 1

#13
cut 18

#13
cut 18

#19
cut 2

[68] *Postage Stamp*

BLOCK ASSEMBLY

#19
cut 9

#19
cut 9

#19
cut 10

#19
cut 8

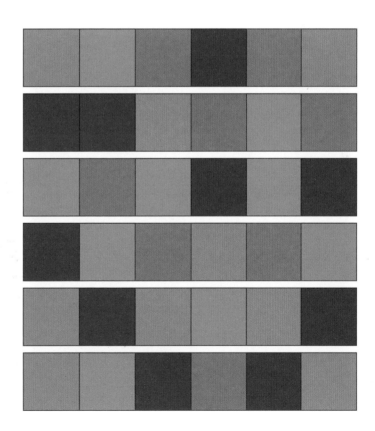

[69] *Practical Orchard*

BLOCK ASSEMBLY

**TEMPLATE NUMBERS &
CUTTING INSTRUCTIONS**

#1
cut 4

#1
cut 4

#20
cut 2

#20
cut 2

[70] *Prairie Queen*

BLOCK ASSEMBLY

**TEMPLATE NUMBERS &
CUTTING INSTRUCTIONS**

#1
cut 1

#3
cut 4

#3
cut 4

#19
cut 8

#19
cut 8

197

[71] *Puss in the Corner*

BLOCK ASSEMBLY

TEMPLATE NUMBERS & CUTTING INSTRUCTIONS

#5
cut 1

#9
cut 4

#7
cut 4

#7
cut 4

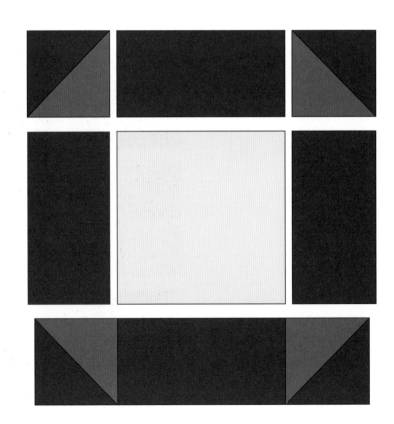

[72] *Railroad*

BLOCK ASSEMBLY

#3
cut 4

#3
cut 4

#19
cut 10

#19
cut 10

[73] *Rainbow Flowers*

BLOCK ASSEMBLY

#17
cut 2

#4
cut 1

#9
cut 2

#4   #4
cut 1   cut 3

#4
cut 1

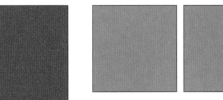

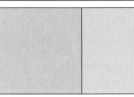

Note: Begin block assembly with the units at the lower right

[74] *Ribbons*

BLOCK ASSEMBLY

**TEMPLATE NUMBERS &
CUTTING INSTRUCTIONS**

#16
cut 4

#16R
cut 4

#7
cut 16

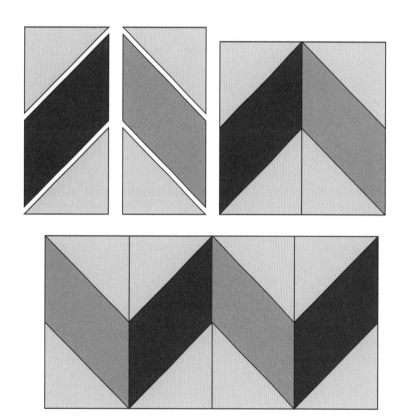

[75] *Rosebud*

BLOCK ASSEMBLY

#13
cut 12

#13
cut 8

#8
cut 4

#3
cut 4

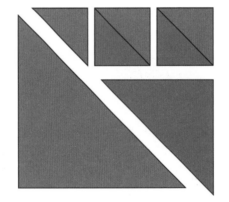

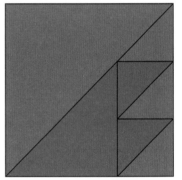

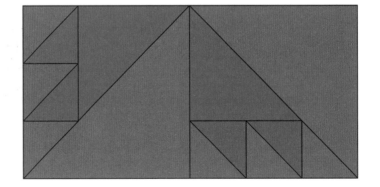

[76] *Sawtooth*

BLOCK ASSEMBLY

#13
cut 11

#13
cut 9

#71
cut 1

#14
cut 1

[77] *Seasons*

BLOCK ASSEMBLY

#73
cut 1

#12
cut 4

#72
cut 4

[78] *Shooting Star*

BLOCK ASSEMBLY

#13
cut 4

#84
cut 4

#54
cut 2

#79
cut 2

#79R
cut 2

#83
cut 2

#83R
cut 2

#23
cut 2

#23R
cut 2

#80
cut 2

#80R
cut 2

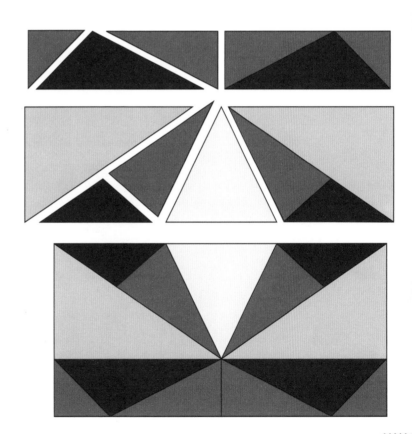

[79] *Silver Lane*

BLOCK ASSEMBLY

TEMPLATE NUMBERS & CUTTING INSTRUCTIONS

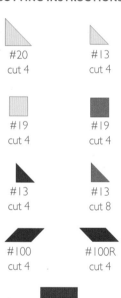

#20
cut 4

#13
cut 4

#19
cut 4

#19
cut 4

#13
cut 4

#13
cut 8

#100
cut 4

#100R
cut 4

#25
cut 4

[80] *Single Wedding Star*

BLOCK ASSEMBLY

TEMPLATE NUMBERS & CUTTING INSTRUCTIONS

#1
cut 1

#21
cut 4

#13
cut 16

#25
cut 4

#25
cut 4

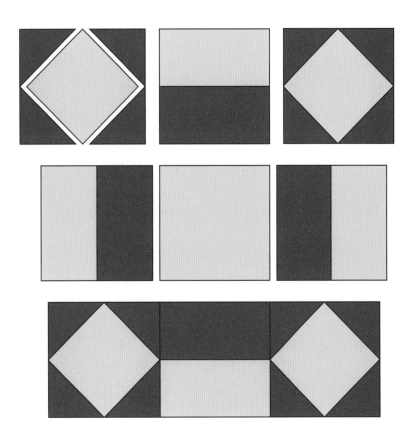

[81] *Snowball*

BLOCK ASSEMBLY

#1
cut 4

#1
cut 1

#3
cut 4

#3
cut 4

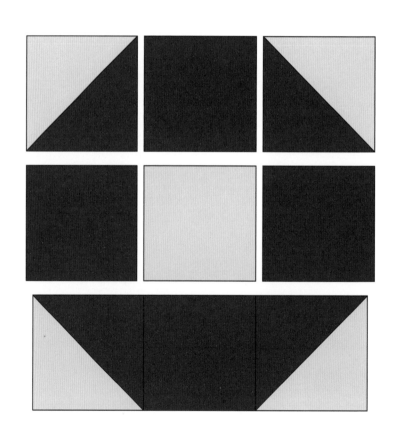

[82] *Spider Legs*

BLOCK ASSEMBLY

TEMPLATE NUMBERS & CUTTING INSTRUCTIONS

#4
cut 1

#85
cut 8

#15
cut 4

#77
cut 4

#77
cut 4

#77R
cut 4

#77R
cut 4

#78
cut 8

[83] *Spider Web*

BLOCK ASSEMBLY

**TEMPLATE NUMBERS &
CUTTING INSTRUCTIONS**

#7
cut 4

#54
cut 4

#86
cut 4

#88
cut 4

#87
cut 4

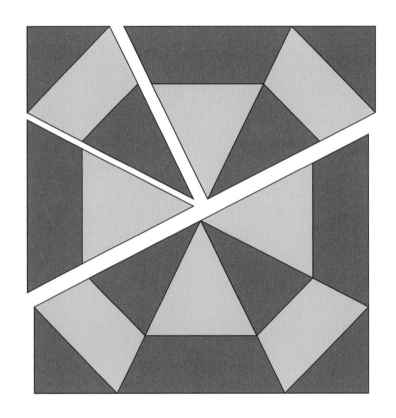

[84] *Spool*

BLOCK ASSEMBLY

#1
cut 3

#1
cut 2

#3
cut 4

#3
cut 4

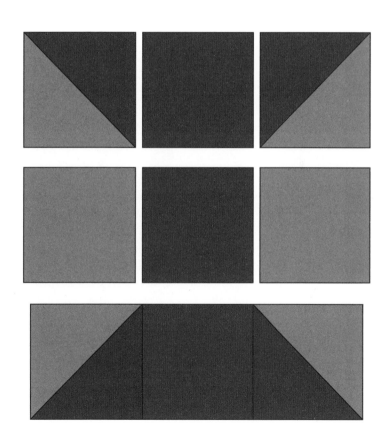

[85] *Square Dance*

TEMPLATE NUMBERS & CUTTING INSTRUCTIONS

#19
cut 4

#82
cut 1

#89
cut 4

#89R
cut 4

#20
cut 4

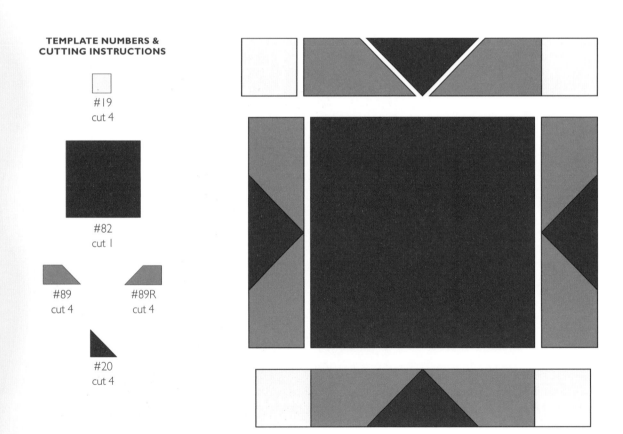

[86] *Squash Blossom*

BLOCK ASSEMBLY

TEMPLATE NUMBERS & CUTTING INSTRUCTIONS

#13
cut 4

#90
cut 2

#90R
cut 2

#89
cut 2

#89R
cut 2

#20
cut 2

#20
cut 2

#91
cut 2

#91R
cut 2

#49
cut 2

[87] *Star Gardener*

BLOCK ASSEMBLY

**TEMPLATE NUMBERS &
CUTTING INSTRUCTIONS**

#19
cut 8

#1
cut 1

#13
cut 24

#13
cut 20

214

[88] *Star of Hope*

BLOCK ASSEMBLY

TEMPLATE NUMBERS & CUTTING INSTRUCTIONS

#34
cut 1

#101
cut 1

#38
cut 8

#38
cut 8

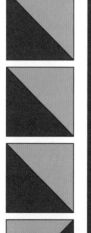

[89] *Steps to the Altar*

BLOCK ASSEMBLY

TEMPLATE NUMBERS & CUTTING INSTRUCTIONS

#1
cut 2

#3
cut 1

#3
cut 2

#19
cut 8

#19
cut 9

#25
cut 2

#13
cut 2

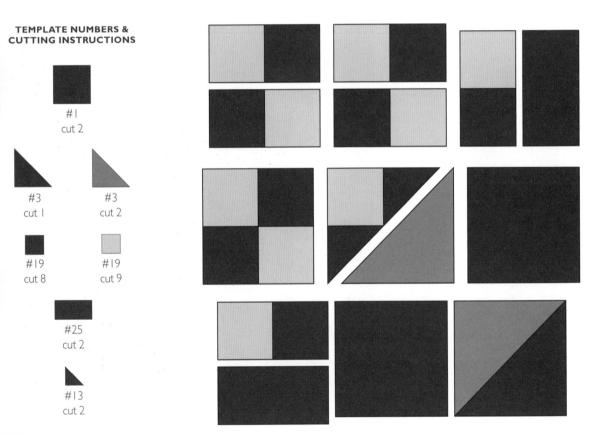

Note: The units in the upper-right and lower-left corners are mirror images

216

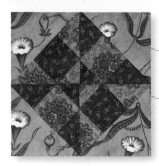

[90] *Storm Signal*

BLOCK ASSEMBLY

#8
cut 4

#20
cut 4

#20
cut 4

#13
cut 2

#13
cut 2

#21
cut 2

#21
cut 2

[91] *Strawberry Basket*

BLOCK ASSEMBLY

#13
cut 4

#1
cut 2

#19
cut 9

#19
cut 9

#3
cut 2

#3
cut 1

#3
cut 1

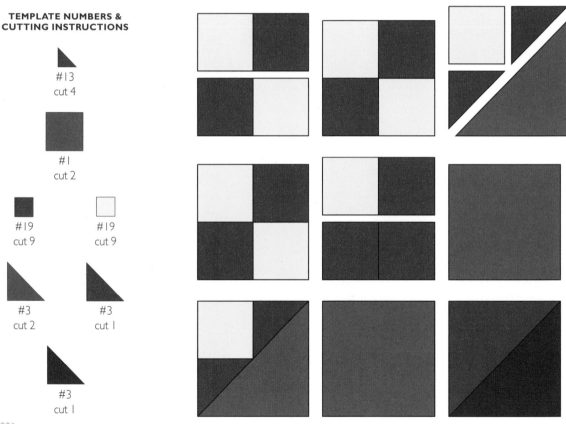

[92] *Streak of Lightning*

BLOCK ASSEMBLY

TEMPLATE NUMBERS & CUTTING INSTRUCTIONS

#19
cut 3

#19
cut 3

#25
cut 8

#25
cut 7

[93] *Swallow*

BLOCK ASSEMBLY

**TEMPLATE NUMBERS &
CUTTING INSTRUCTIONS**

#5
cut 1

#7
cut 10

#7
cut 7

#76
cut 1

#76R
cut 1

#4
cut 2

#102
cut 1

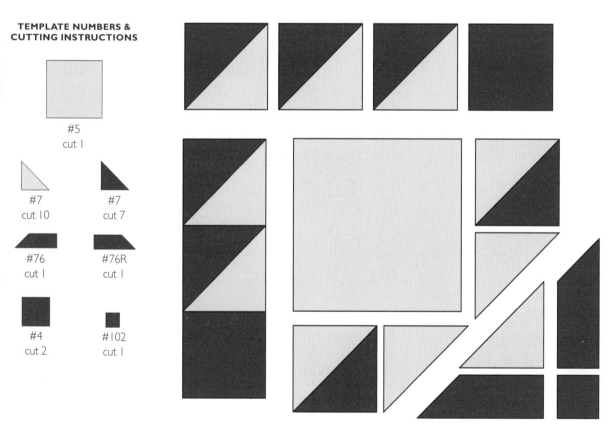

Note: Begin block assembly in lower-right corner

[94] *Tall Pine Tree*

BLOCK ASSEMBLY

**TEMPLATE NUMBERS &
CUTTING INSTRUCTIONS**

#74
cut 4

#74R
cut 4

#74
cut 4

#74R
cut 4

#75
cut 4

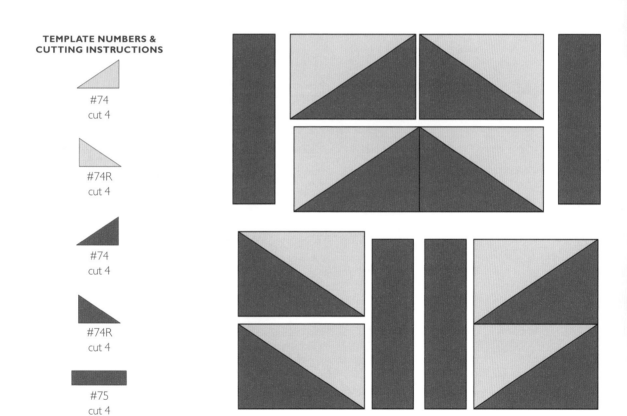

[95] *Temperance Tree*

BLOCK ASSEMBLY

**TEMPLATE NUMBERS &
CUTTING INSTRUCTIONS**

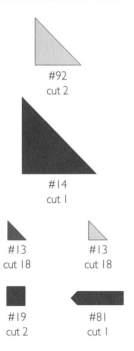

#92
cut 2

#14
cut 1

#13
cut 18

#13
cut 18

#19
cut 2

#81
cut 1

BLOCK ASSEMBLY

TEMPLATE NUMBERS & CUTTING INSTRUCTIONS

#8
cut 1

#45
cut 1

#45
cut 1

#16
cut 1

#16R
cut 1

#93
cut 1

#4
cut 1

#93R
cut 1

#7
cut 6

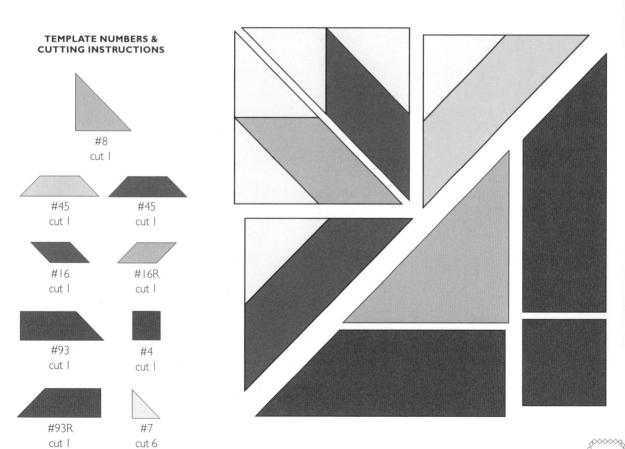

[97] *Waste Not*

BLOCK ASSEMBLY

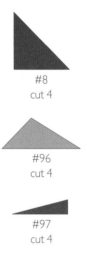

#8
cut 4

#96
cut 4

#97
cut 4

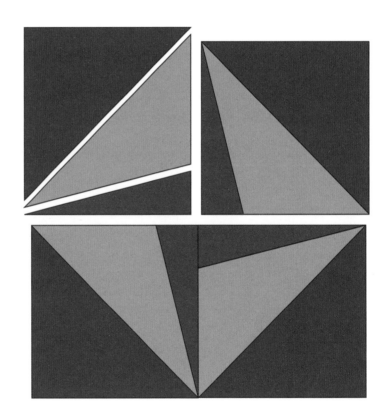

[98] *Waterwheel*

**TEMPLATE NUMBERS &
CUTTING INSTRUCTIONS**

#3
cut 2

#3
cut 4

#3
cut 2

#19
cut 4

#19
cut 8

#19
cut 4

#19
cut 4

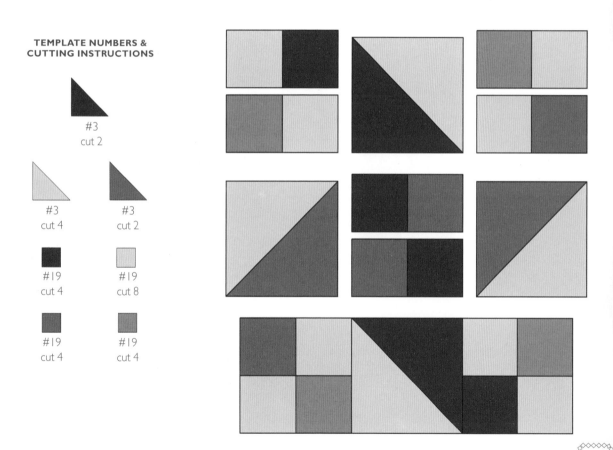

[99] *W.C.T.U.*

BLOCK ASSEMBLY

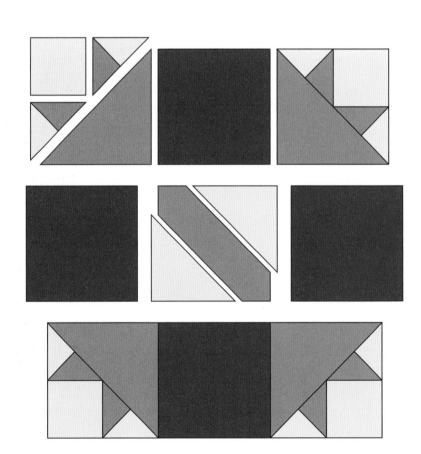

[100] *Weathervane*

BLOCK ASSEMBLY

#19
cut 4

#1
cut 1

#20
cut 4

#20
cut 8

#13
cut 16

#25
cut 4

[101] *Wedding Ring*

BLOCK ASSEMBLY

TEMPLATE NUMBERS & CUTTING INSTRUCTIONS

#34
cut 4

#34
cut 5

#38
cut 4

#38
cut 16

#38
cut 8

#38
cut 4

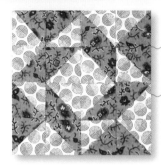

[102] *Whirlpool*

BLOCK ASSEMBLY

TEMPLATE NUMBERS & CUTTING INSTRUCTIONS

#7
cut 16

#7
cut 16

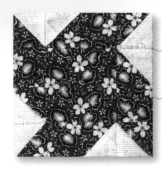

[103] *Whirlwind*

BLOCK ASSEMBLY

#4
cut 4

#5
cut 1

#7
cut 8

#7
cut 8

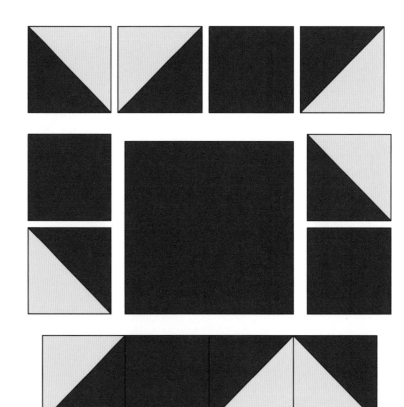

[104] *Wild Geese*

BLOCK ASSEMBLY

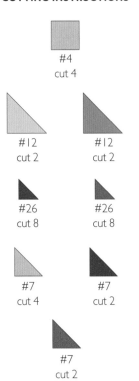

#4
cut 4

#12
cut 2

#12
cut 2

#26
cut 8

#26
cut 8

#7
cut 4

#7
cut 2

#7
cut 2

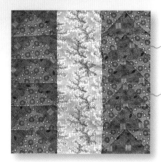

[105] *Wild Goose Chase*

BLOCK ASSEMBLY

TEMPLATE NUMBERS & CUTTING INSTRUCTIONS

#94
cut 1

#20
cut 6

#20
cut 6

#13
cut 12

#13
cut 12

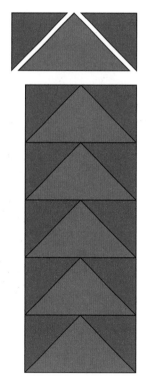

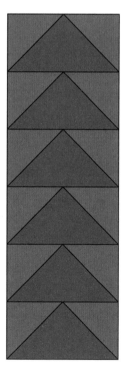

[106] *Wild Rose & Square*

BLOCK ASSEMBLY

TEMPLATE NUMBERS & CUTTING INSTRUCTIONS

#34
cut 1

#34
cut 8

#34
cut 4

#38
cut 8

#38
cut 8

#38
cut 8

[107] *Windblown Square*

BLOCK ASSEMBLY

#7
cut 16

#7
cut 8

#7
cut 8

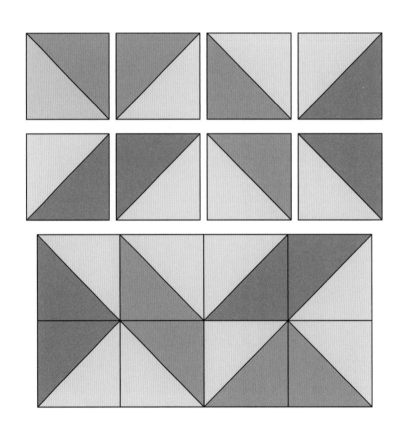

[108] *Windmill*

BLOCK ASSEMBLY

TEMPLATE NUMBERS & CUTTING INSTRUCTIONS

#98
cut 4

#99
cut 1

#99
cut 1

#99
cut 1

#99
cut 1

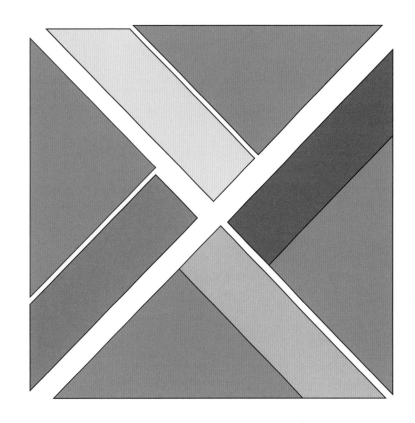

[109] *Windows*

BLOCK ASSEMBLY

#12
cut 2

#12
cut 2

#95
cut 2

#9
cut 2

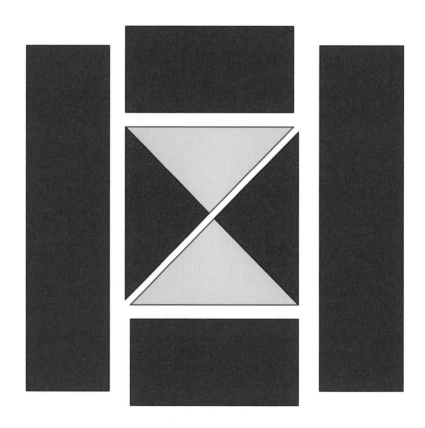

[110] *Wood Lily*

BLOCK ASSEMBLY

#21
cut 1

#20
cut 4

#20
cut 12

#77
cut 4

#77R
cut 4

#77
cut 8

#77R
cut 8

#13
cut 8

#85
cut 8

[111] *Wrench*

BLOCK ASSEMBLY

#1
cut 1

#3
cut 4

#3
cut 4

#25
cut 4

#25
cut 4

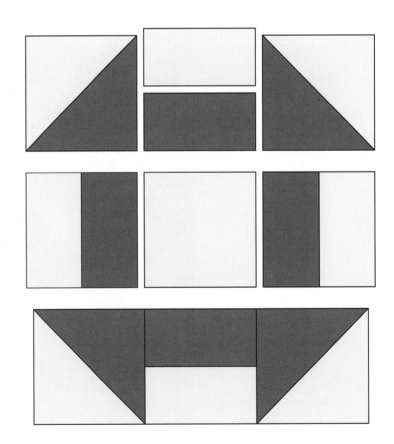

Quilt Assembly

Refer to the quilt assembly diagrams on pages 245-248 for the number of blocks in each row for the size quilt you are making.

BLOCK ROWS

1 Begin a row with each setting triangle (template 71). Alternate sashing strips (template 106) with blocks.

2 End each row with a setting triangle (template 71).

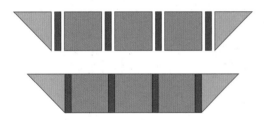

SASHING ROWS

1 Begin the row with a little triangle (template 13). Alternate sashing strips (template 106) and cornerstones (template 19). End with a little triangle (template 13).

JOIN ROWS

1 Sew a sashing row to the top of each block row.

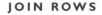

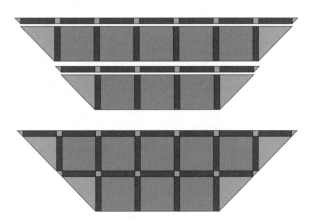

QUILT CORNERS

Regardless of size, each quilt has this unit in its upper-left and lower-right corners.

1 Sew sashing strips (template 106), followed by triangles (template 71), to one side of each upper-left and lower-right block.

2 Make a short sashing row and sew it to the top of the block row. Add a small setting triangle (template 22) to the top. The lower-left and upper-right corners are formed by adding setting triangles to the ends of the rows.

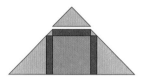

3 For a king-size quilt, sew small setting triangles (template 22) to each end of the quilt's center diagonal row.

4 For the lower-left corner of a queen, twin or lap quilt, sew a small setting triangle (template 22) to the left side of the row and a large setting triangle (template 71) to the right side of the row.

5 For the upper-right corner of a queen, twin or lap quilt, sew a large setting triangle (template 71) to the left side of the row and a small setting triangle (template 22) to the right side of the row.

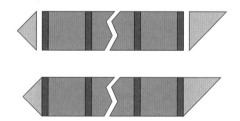

6 Join the rows according to the quilt assembly diagram for lap-, twin-, queen- or king-size quilt (pages 245–248).

ADDING A BORDER

1 Cut border strips as indicated in fabric requirements and cutting instructions for appropriate quilt size (pages 245-248). Join strips end to end.

2 To determine the length of the top and bottom borders, measure the quilt width through the center.

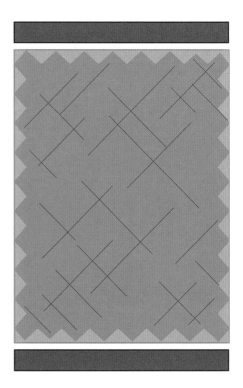

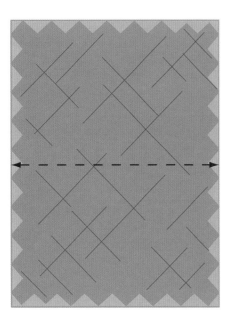

3 From the joined strips, cut 2 strips to the length determined in step 2. Sew these to the top and bottom of the quilt.

4 To determine the length of the side borders, measure the quilt length, including the top and bottom borders, through the center.

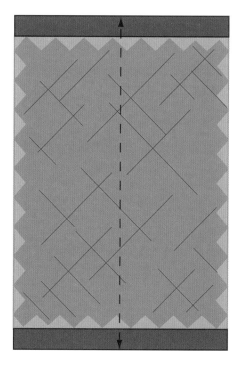

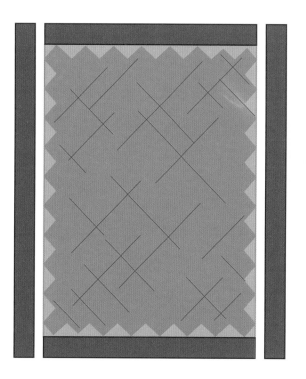

5 Cut 2 strips the length determined in step 4. Sew one strip to each side of the quilt.

FINISHING THE QUILT

1 Piece the backing according to the instructions for the appropriate quilt size.

Lap quilt (57½" x 67½"): Cut 3¾ yards of backing fabric into two 67½" pieces. Join the two pieces lengthwise, as shown.

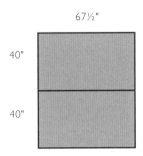

67½"

40"

40"

Twin quilt (73" x 92½"): Cut 5¾ yards into two pieces, 2⅞ yards each. Cut one of the pieces in half lengthwise. Join the three pieces lengthwise.

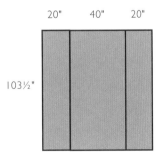

20" 40" 20"

103½"

Queen quilt (83" x 103") and King quilt (103" x 103"): Cut 9½ yards into three pieces, 114" each. Join the pieces lengthwise.

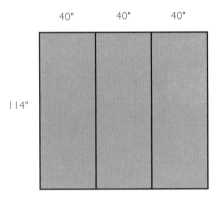

40" 40" 40"

114"

2 Layer a "quilt sandwich" beginning with the backing wrong side up, batting, and then the quilt top right side up.

3 Baste or pin the layers together, and quilt as desired.

4 Trim excess batting and backing.

5 Sew binding strips end-to-end, then apply the binding to the quilt as desired.

Lap-Size Quilt

There are III block designs to choose from in this book. Pick your favorite 50 to make a lap-size quilt.

QUILT SIZE

57" × 67"

BLOCK SIZE

6" × 6"

FABRIC REQUIREMENTS

Muslin: 1 yard

Brown: 2¼ yards

Backing: 3¾ yards

Batting: 63" × 73"

Based on a 40" width of fabric, cut the following:

From Muslin, cut:

- 40 cornerstones (template 19)

- 22 little setting triangles (template 13)

- 18 large setting triangles (template 71)

- 4 small setting triangles (template 22)

From Brown, cut:

- 120 sashing strips (template 106)

- 6 border strips 4" × 40"

- 7 binding strips 2½" × 40"

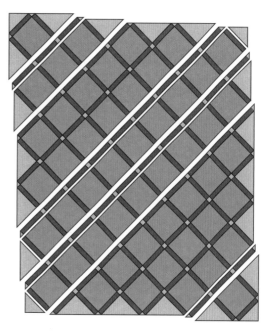

Lap-Size Quilt Assembly

The CD-ROM contains a larger, printable version of this diagram.

Twin-Size Sampler Quilt

There are 111 block designs to choose from in this book.
Pick your favorite 83 blocks to make a twin-size quilt.

QUILT SIZE

73" × 92½"

BLOCK SIZE:

6" × 6"

FABRIC REQUIREMENTS

Muslin: 1¼ yards

Brown: 4 yards

Backing: 5¾ yards

Batting: 79" × 98½"

Based on a 40" width of fabric, cut the following:

From Muslin, cut:

- 82 cornerstones (template 19)
- 28 little setting triangles (template 13)
- 24 large setting triangles (template 71)
- 4 small setting triangles (template 22)

From Brown, cut:

- 192 sashing strips (template 106)
- 8 border strips 7" × 40"
- 9 binding strips 2½" × 40"

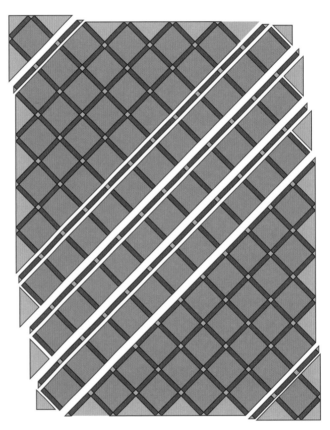

Twin-Size Quilt Assembly

The CD-ROM contains a larger, printable version of this diagram.

Queen-Size Sampler Quilt

I chose to make a queen-size sampler quilt (pictured on page 239). Originally, I made 110 blocks—two blocks for each letter. When I arranged the finished blocks into rows, something didn't look right. Then I tried setting the blocks on point, and the quilt came alive. The on-point arrangement required one more block. Rather than play favorites with one of the block designs, I added one more.

QUILT SIZE

83" × 103"

BLOCK SIZE

6" × 6"

FABRIC REQUIREMENTS

Muslin: 1½ yards

Brown: 4¾ yards

Backing: 9½ yards

Batting: 89" × 109"

Based on a 40" width of fabric, cut the following:

From Muslin, cut:

- 110 cornerstones (template 19)
- 32 little setting triangles (template 13)
- 28 large setting triangles (template 71)
- 4 small setting triangles (template 22)

From Brown, cut:

- 252 sashing strips (template 106)
- 9 border strips 7" × 40"
- 10 binding strips 2½" × 40"

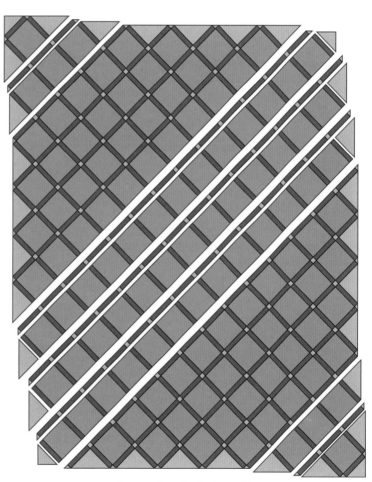

Queen-Size Quilt Assembly

The CD-ROM contains a larger, printable version of this diagram.

King-Size Sampler Quilt

There are 111 block designs to choose from in this book. To make a king-size quilt, you'll need 145 blocks. Repeat 34 of the blocks or use other traditional block patterns of your own choice.

QUILT SIZE

103" × 103"

BLOCK SIZE

6" × 6"

FABRIC REQUIREMENTS

Muslin: 1½ yards

Brown: 5⅜ yards

Backing: 9½ yards

Batting: 109" × 109"

Based on a 40" width of fabric, cut the following:

From Muslin, cut:

- 144 cornerstones (template 19)

- 36 little setting triangles (template 13)

- 32 large setting triangles (template 71)

- 4 small setting triangles (template 22)

From Brown, cut:

- 324 sashing strips (template 106)

- 10 border strips 7" × 40"

- 12 binding strips 2½" × 40"

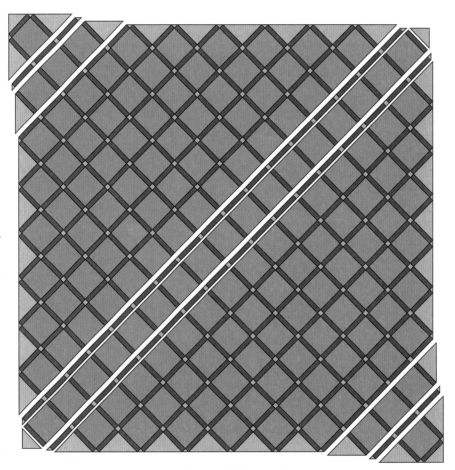

King-Size Quilt Assembly

The CD-ROM contains a larger, printable version of this diagram.

Contest Winners
IN ORDER OF PUBLICATION

FIRST PLACE:
Mrs. Fannie L. Brundage,
Fairfield County, Connecticut

SECOND PLACE:
Annette C. Dimock,
Orange County, Vermont

THIRD PLACE:
Mrs. Cola L. Fountain,
Jefferson County, New York

HONORABLE MENTIONS

Mrs. J. B.,
Polk County, Wisconsin

Mrs. G. B. S.,
Saline County, Missouri

E. M. W.,
Dukes County, Masschusetts

M. P. E.,
Nodaway County, Missouri

Mrs. I. L. M.,
Prince Georges County, Maryland

C. P. G.,
Berkeley County, West Virginia

Mrs. W. S. B.,
Mills County, Iowa

Mrs. B. G.,
Delaware County, Ohio

Mrs. F. W. C.,
Chautauqua County, New York

Mrs. G. W. N.,
Ingham County, Michigan

Mrs. E. M. L.,
Furnas County, Nebraska

Mrs. J. M V.,
Pocahontas County, Iowa

Mrs. G. B. H.,
Richland County, Montana

Mrs. L. H. D.,
Worcester County, Masschusetts

Mrs. A. B .D.,
Park County, Wyoming

E. H.,
Riley County, Kansas

Mrs. J. J. T.,
Cascade County, Montana

Mrs. F. Y. K.,
Hawkins County, Tennessee

M. R. G.,
Roanoke County, Virginia

Mrs. G. R. B.,
Wood County, West Virginia

R. B. B.,
Lee County, Iowa

Mrs. A. U.,
Ransom County, North Dakota

Mrs. G. R. E.,
Morgan County, Alabama

Mrs. C. B.,
Jefferson County, Wisconsin

Mrs. E. A. E.,
Chenango County, New York

Mrs. H. U.,
Grand Forks County, North Dakota

Mrs. J. E. F.,
Valley County, Montana

E. S.,
Milwaukee County, Wisconsin

Mrs. C. R. M.,
Ramsey County, North Dakota

Mrs. A. B.,
Marion County, Kansas

C. Mc. D. B.,
Marion County, Indiana

Mrs. M. M. C.,
Allegheny County, Pennsylvania

Mrs. E. F.,
Clay County, Indiana

Mrs. H. M. C.,
Lawrence County, South Dakota

M. E. T.,
Hennepin County, Minnesota

Mrs. I. G.,
Sauk County, Wisconsin

Mrs. W. R.,
Hutchinson County, South Dakota

Mrs. L. C. F.,
Montcalm County, Michigan

Mrs. O. D. G.,
Coshocton County, Ohio

Mrs. C. R. E.,
Rio Grande County, Colorado

Mrs. C. K. T.,
Newton County, Indiana

Mrs. C. B. H.,
Clay County, Mississippi

Mrs. R. A. S.,
Shawnee County, Kansas

Mrs. M. A. D.,
Sargent County, North Dakota

Mrs. R. C. W.,
Jasper County, Missouri

Mrs. C. F. C.,
Chautauqua County, New York

Mrs. J. A. M.,
Ingham County, Michigan

Mrs. J. R. F.,
Canadian County, Oklahoma

Mrs. H. St. C.,
Franklin County, Iowa

Mrs. D. N.,
Grady County, Oklahoma

Mrs. S. O.,
Mille Lacs County, Minnesota

Mrs. N. M. M.,
Westchester County, New York

Mrs. I. C.,
Harrison County, Iowa

Mrs. E. F.,
Portage County, Wisconsin

Mrs. W. B. McC.,
Fulton County, Ohio

Mrs. J. W. P.,
Platt County, Illinois

Mrs. C. L. C.,
Tuscola County, Michigan

Mrs. S. M. M.,
Franklin County, Ohio

Mrs. C. E. S.,
Lee County, Illinois

Mrs. C. M. B.,
Cheshire County, New Hampshire

Mrs. H. J. N.,
Nevada County, California

Mrs. M. H. M.,
Charlotte County, Virginia

W. C. W.,
Iredell County, North Carolina

Mrs. A. C. C.,
Audubon County, Iowa

Mrs. C. A. B.,
Garfield County, Oklahoma

For reasons unknown to the author, the editors of *The Farmer's Wife* magazine chose not to give the full names of the contest winners, with the exception of the first, second and third place winners. If you know the identity of any of these women, the author would love to hear their stories. Please contact her at thefarmerswifequilt@yahoo.com.

NOTES

[1] **Bonheur, Rosa** (1822-1899). A Realist, she was considered the most famous female painter of the 1800s.

[2] **Farm Bureau.** Founded in 1919, it serves as an educational and legislative organization to further the concerns of farmers.

[3] **Flapper.** A younger woman, especially in the 1920s, who showed disdain for conventional dress and behavior.

[4] **Flivvers.** Slang for an old, small and cheap automobile.

[5] **Rural Free Delivery** (RFD). Before this service began in 1891, residents of rural areas had to go into town to pick up their mail. Rural folks received a further boost when parcel post delivery began in 1913. Magazines, non-local newspapers—and more importantly—the whole world of the mail-order catalog was now open to the farmer and his wife.

[6] **Galli-Curci, Amelita** (1899-1963). An Italian-born operatic soprano; she was regarded as one of the best in the early 1900s.

[7] **Gluck, Alma** (1884-1938). A Rumanian-born soprano, and mother of actor Efrem Zimbalist, Jr.

[8] **The Grange.** The common name of the Order of Patrons of Husbandry was organized in the South in 1867. It is a fraternal organization for men and women, founded on the model of the Masonic Order. The members are "united by the strong and faithful tie of Agriculture."

[9] **Jitney.** A small bus that carries passengers over a regular route.

[10] **Kreisler, Fritz** (1875-1962). An Austrian violinist and composer who later became a U.S. citizen. He was one of the most famous violinists of his day.

[11] **Rubens, Peter Paul** (1577-1640). Flemish painter of the Baroque style

[12] **Ruskin, John** (1819-1900). An English reformer, critic and writer

[13] **Sifton, Sir Clifford** (1861-1929). A Canadian politician who was instrumental in encouraging the mass immigration to Canada in the very early twentieth century.

[14] **Skat.** A three-handed card game played with thirty-two cards.

[15] **Sousa, John Philip** (1854-1932). Known as the "March King," he was an American-born bandmaster and composer.

[16] **Vamping.** Practicing seductive wiles on men.

[17] **Van Dyke, Henry** (1852-1933). An American author, poet and educator. The quotation is from his poem "The Three Best Things."

[18] **Victrola.** The most popular brand of home phonograph. The Victor Talking Machine Company (1901–1929) began manufacturing them in 1906.

[19] **W.C.T.U.** The Women's Christian Temperance Union was founded in 1874. It spearheaded the crusade for prohibition.

ABOUT THE AUTHOR

In her childhood, Laurie Aaron Hird loved reading books about the pioneers and has always wished that she had been born during those quieter days. It has been a struggle at times, but she has learned to live in two worlds—one with her wood cookstove and clothesline, and the other, less cozy, world with her cell phone and a computer. Laurie taught herself to quilt and especially enjoys working with reproduction fabrics and collecting photographs of antique quilts. She is happily living with her family on six acres in rural southwest Wisconsin, where they homeschool, maintain a kitchen garden and take care of their animals.

INDEX

254

Every quilt has a story to tell…

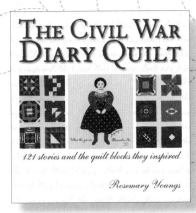

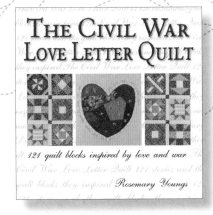

THE CIVIL WAR DIARY QUILT

Rosemary Youngs

Bring the past alive with distinctive, exquisite quilt blocks that tell the stories of 10 women living and surviving the Civil War. Explore the diary entries of these women, plus instructions for 121 related quilt blocks.

paperback; 8" × 8"; 288 pages
ISBN-10: 0-87349-995-6
ISBN-13: 978-0-87349-995-8
SRN: CWQD

THE CIVIL WAR LOVE LETTER QUILT

Rosemary Youngs

Get wrapped up in the lives and loves of 11 Civil War soldiers and the beautiful quilt their stories inspired. Using 121 different blocks, you can create any of the 14 projects, including a full-size quilt, lap quilts, wall hangings and table runners.

paperback; 8" × 8"; 288 pages
ISBN-10: 0-89689-487-8
ISBN-13: 978-0-89689-487-7
SRN: Z0751